THE
1916
DIARIES

OF AN IRISH REBEL
AND A BRITISH SOLDIER

THE
1916
DIARIES

OF AN IRISH REBEL
AND A BRITISH SOLDIER

Mick O'Farrell

MERCIER PRESS
IRISH PUBLISHER – IRISH STORY

DEDICATED TO CONOR, EVE AND AMANDA
(*FAMILIA MEA, UXOR MEA, VITA MEA*).
THANKS FOR PUTTING UP WITH THE SMELLY
BOOKS!

MERCIER PRESS

Cork

www.mercierpress.ie

© Mick O'Farrell, 2014

ISBN: 978 1 78117 244 5

10 9 8 7 6 5 4 3 2 1

A CIP record for this title is available from the British Library

Printed and bound in the EU.

CONTENTS

Acknowledgements

Thanks to the following for content, permissions, and assistance: Aengus Ó Snodaigh, TD; Pádraig Ó Snodaigh; Colm Ó Snodaigh; Commandant Pádraic Kennedy, Military Archives; Rebecca Newell, National Army Museum; Douglas Appleyard; Tom Morrissey, SJ; Ray Bateson; Gerry Gibson; and Stephen Brophy, Department of Arts, Heritage and the Gaeltacht.

Thanks also to Una Byrne O'Carroll, daughter of Agnes and granddaughter of Seosamh de Brún and Ann Walsh; to Jim Rocliffe, son-in-law of Agnes; to Lorraine Rocliffe Bridgette, granddaughter of Agnes; and to Sean Ó Broin, grandson of Seosamh de Brún and source of much de Brún family history.

Many thanks to Derek Jones for *Thoms* and the rest; to Karl Vines, whose photographs finally made it into print; and to Mary Feehan and the team at Mercier Press.

Special thanks to Ursula O'Farrell for helping with tiny handwriting, to Ursula Byrne (UCD Library) for providing access to obscurity and to Denis O'Farrell for careful digitisation of a delicate diary.

occurrence, the use of any material is a breach of copyright, I apologise sincerely and will be more than happy to incorporate the relevant notice in future reprints or editions of this book.

INTRODUCTION

This book isn't an account of the 1916 Easter Rising as a whole – it's not even a detailed record of a single garrison. Instead it's a tightly focused look at events as they happened to two individuals who were deeply involved in the rebellion, but on different sides – an Irish Volunteer in Jacob's factory and a British soldier in Dublin's city centre.

In their own way, both Seosamh de Brún and Samuel H. Lomas were quite ordinary men, living unspectacular lives. In April 1916, one was thirty-two years old and the other thirty-six, with the potential for many more ordinary years ahead of them. But during that month both men found themselves in action on the streets of Dublin, taking part on opposing sides of Ireland's Easter rebellion. Before the month was over, both underwent life-changing experiences, and one had no idea that he had less than a year to live, before dying on a battlefield in France. Up to that point though, there's still nothing particularly unusual or outstanding about their stories – after all, large numbers of men shared the fighting on Dublin's streets in 1916.

What sets these two men apart for later generations is what they did during the rebellion's quiet moments – they both kept personal diaries, recording for themselves (and fortunately for posterity) the sights they saw and the actions they experienced.

There are of course other diaries available which were

written by British soldiers during the Rising, but until now Company Sergeant Major Lomas' account has only been available via London's National Army Museum. Like many diaries written during major historical upheavals, it's an account filled with both the fascinating and the humdrum – from 'Had dinner and a short rest' to the fact that Tom Clarke required 'a bullet from the officer to complete the business'.

Volunteer Seosamh de Brún's diary, on the other hand, is unique among accounts of the Easter Rising – it's the only known diary kept by an ordinary Volunteer under fire. Naturally it too contains the fascinating and the humdrum, but along the way it reveals what an 'ordinary' rebel was experiencing during Easter Week – not only do we get a first-hand, unadulterated version of the events and the history he was part of, but we also get a glimpse into the mindset of a Volunteer who 'did not expect to be involved in Revolution at least so suddenly'. And because he kept the diary from late 1915, we even come to know something of de Brún's circumstances in the months before the Rising – not just the hard times he was going through, with a drastic shortage of work and wages, but also the problems he was having within his company of Volunteers: 'B. Coy. Coldness. The limit reached. Left early.'

Despite his personal difficulties, and an apparent disillusionment with the Volunteer organisation, de Brún responded immediately and enthusiastically to the rebel mobilisation on Monday 24 April: 'We believe we are going to make a sacrifice. We offer it to god & our country.' Later in the week he was one of just fourteen Volunteers who left Jacob's on bicycle to try to relieve the pressure on Éamon de Valera's position near Mount Street – one man was fatally wounded, and de Brún, on his return, opened his diary and wrote: 'I did not think I would return.'

Thirty-three years later, de Brún wrote again of his rebellion experiences when he gave a statement to the Bureau of Military History in 1949. By then he had the luxury of taking time to consider and even compose his recollections – his statement is reproduced in full here, and provides a fascinating comparison to the small scribbled notes written in a tiny pocket diary all those years earlier.

Now, of course, Seosamh de Brún's diary is almost 100 years old, and it's a privilege to be able to finally share it with the public before it reaches its own centenary. I first wrote about the 1916 Rising in 1999, and back then I said: '... in a matter of months from now, the Easter Rising will be viewed through a new lens ... it will become something that happened "last century". Inevitably, people's perception ... will alter simply because of the change in date ...'.[1] Perceptions may indeed have altered, but thankfully time has shown that the public's interest in this momentous event in Ireland's history hasn't diminished, and an encouraging number of books and new research into the rebellion have continued to be produced. Now another potential shift in perception is fast approaching – as 2016 comes and goes, the Rising will become something

1   O'Farrell, M., *A Walk Through Rebel Dublin*, p. 6

that happened over a hundred years ago. It will have moved from something merely old to something from long ago. Nevertheless, the historian's hope remains the same – that interest in the uprising will continue to grow, and that more books and more research on the subject will be published. There will of course be the inevitable flurry of books on the subject (including this one) in the run-up to the Rising's centenary, but, as the rediscovery of Volunteer de Brún's diary, as well as the recent release of Military Pensions information shows, nearly 100 years on there are still fresh sources to be uncovered and mined, so we can hopefully look forward to fresh approaches and fresh studies of the Easter Rising well into the post-centenary years.

With that in mind, I'll end by re-making the appeal I made in 1999: 'There are accounts existing which, although written down, have never been published, and there are also oral testimonies passed on and still remembered – I would appeal to anyone with such testimonies in their possession or their memory to do whatever they can to make them publicly available.'

Mick O'Farrell, Dublin, 2014

Note:

When quoting from a direct source, I've retained the spelling of certain words as they were originally used – for example, McDermott instead of MacDermott, Feinners instead of Féiners, etc. Also, references are made to both Sackville Street and O'Connell

Street – they are of course the same street. Although in 1916 its official name was Sackville Street, many nationalist writers of the time referred to it by its unofficial title, O'Connell Street, and both names were to a degree acceptable. In May 1924, forty years after the original motion was actually carried in 1884, a meeting of Dublin Corporation adopted the motion 'That the name of Sackville Street be, and it is hereby, changed to O'Connell Street' in accordance with Section 42 of the Dublin Corporation Act, 1890.

The Easter Rising, Day By Day

Apart from some small actions, the 1916 Rising lasted seven days, from Easter Monday to the following Sunday.

Easter Monday, 24 April 1916

Beginning of the rebellion. The main body of rebels musters outside Liberty Hall – conflicting orders result in a turnout much smaller than hoped for. From about midday on, the following locations are occupied by rebels:

- GPO and other buildings in Sackville Street area
- Four Courts, Mendicity Institution
- St Stephen's Green, College of Surgeons
- Boland's Mill and surrounding area, including Mount Street Bridge and nearby houses
- City Hall and several buildings overlooking Dublin Castle
- Jacob's biscuit factory, Davy's pub by Portobello Bridge
- South Dublin Union and James's Street area
- Magazine Fort in Phoenix Park.

The Proclamation of the Republic is read by Pearse outside the GPO. Lancers charge down Sackville Street. Looting starts. That afternoon, the British counterattacks begin.

Tuesday, 25 April 1916

City Hall is retaken by the military. Shelbourne Hotel is

occupied by soldiers and machine-gun fire forces rebels to retreat to the College of Surgeons. British reinforcements, including artillery, arrive. Martial law is proclaimed in Dublin city and county.

Wednesday, 26 April 1916

Liberty Hall is shelled by the gunboat *Helga*, backed by field guns. Artillery is put into action against buildings on Sackville Street. Kelly's Fort is evacuated. The Metropole Hotel is occupied by rebels. Troops marching from Dun Laoghaire are halted by rebels at Mount Street Bridge. After many hours of intense fighting and terrible casualties, the military gain control of the area. Clanwilliam House burns to the ground. The Mendicity Institution is retaken by the British. Martial law is proclaimed throughout Ireland.

Thursday, 27 April 1916

Military shelling of Sackville Street intensifies. Fires on Sackville Street begin to rage out of control. Hopkins & Hopkins and the Imperial Hotel are evacuated because of the inferno.

Friday, 28 April 1916

General Sir John Maxwell arrives in Dublin. The Metropole Hotel is evacuated. Rebels evacuate the GPO and establish a new HQ in Moore Street.

Saturday, 29 April 1916

Non-combatants are murdered in North King Street. Rebel

leaders in Moore Street decide to surrender. The Four Courts' garrison surrenders.

Sunday, 30 April 1916

Rebels in remaining outposts surrender – College of Surgeons; Boland's; Jacob's; South Dublin Union. Deportations begin – eventually over 3,000 people arrested in connection with the rebellion are sent to prison in England.

Wednesday, 3 May–Friday, 12 May 1916

Fifteen rebels, including the seven signatories of the Proclamation of the Republic, are executed by firing squad.

'Some Wrote Diaries of Events to Date ...'

An introduction to Seosamh de Brún, 'B' Company, 2nd Battalion, Dublin Brigade Irish Volunteers

Battered and worn, the diary of Seosamh de Brún is a 'Collins' Midget Diary for 1916' – a very small pocket diary, measuring not quite 7 x 6 centimetres (3 x 2¼ inches), with a well-worn red cover. This is what de Brún wrote in and carried with him from late 1915 to Saturday 29 April 1916. He made regular entries in his diary during that time,

A picture of the outside cover of the diary of Seosamh de Brún, actual size.

writing about not just his personal circumstances, but about the difficulties he was having finding work and his trade union membership, among other things.

From an historical point of view though, the most interesting notes in de Brún's diary relate to his membership of another organisation – the Irish Volunteers. We don't know all the details of his membership, but we do know that he joined at the organisation's inception, that he was very active in the Volunteers throughout 1916 and that he served in Jacob's factory during the Easter Rising, with his diary entries ending abruptly after a note which seems to have been written towards the end of Saturday, 29 April. The garrison within Jacob's surrendered the next day, 30 April.

De Brún wasn't among the Volunteers who surrendered, but in an account of the rebellion that he gave some thirty-three years later, he wrote: 'Numbers of the men were given the option to escape from the building and availed of it.'[1] From the same account we also know that de Brún was wearing his Volunteer uniform, which he calls his 'service rig', and since it's unlikely that he could have avoided capture in uniform, we can suppose that at some point after Commandant Thomas MacDonagh announced the surrender of the Jacob's garrison, de Brún shed his uniform before merging into the crowd that was then surrounding the building.[2]

Also around this time, de Brún was separated from his diary – perhaps it fell out of his pocket while he changed

1   Seosamh de Brún, Bureau of Military History Witness Statement (BMH WS) 312, p. 18.
2   Thomas MacDonagh was a signatory of the Proclamation of the Republic and commandant of the Volunteers' 2nd Battalion, Dublin Brigade. He was executed by firing squad on 3 May by soldiers of the 2/6 Battalion, the Sherwood Foresters, with Company Sergeant Major S. H. Lomas serving as senior NCO at the execution – see p. 185.

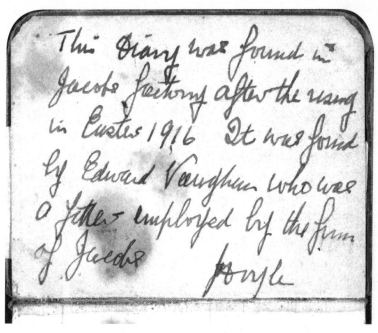

An image of the inside back cover of the diary.

into civilian clothes, or maybe he left it behind in the pocket of his Volunteer uniform. Interestingly, in his 1949 account he mentions that he still possesses a razor that he had used on the Sunday morning, so we know he did deliberately save some items. Nevertheless, since he never mentioned the diary's existence again, de Brún himself offers no clues as to how it came to be left behind, so we'll probably never know the full story. What we do know is that the diary was subsequently found after the Rising had ended – a note written inside the back cover was added in a new hand, saying: 'This diary was found in Jacobs factory after the rising in Easter 1916. It was found by Edward

Vaughan[3] who was a fitter employed by the firm of Jacobs – J Doyle.'[4]

In his 1949 statement de Brún mentions, almost in passing, that while at rest, 'the men reclined, smoked, read and chatted, some wrote diaries of events to date.' This is intriguing for two reasons – firstly, he had either forgotten entirely about his own diary, or he was making an oblique reference to it, presuming it to be lost (de Brún's family knew nothing of the diary's existence until it was rediscovered in the last few years). Secondly, and perhaps more interesting for the historian, he raises the prospect that there may be other diaries by Jacob's Volunteers still to be uncovered after nearly 100 years. Certainly, it's extremely unlikely that rebels in other besieged garrisons had time to put pen to paper – the relative quiet of Jacob's probably provided the only opportunity for such reflection. In any case, de Brún's 1916 diary is, for the moment at least, the only known diary of the Easter Rising by a rank and file Volunteer.

Seosamh de Brún was born on 3 July 1883, the eldest son of James and Jane Brown. At the 1901 census the Browns had seven sons, from two to seventeen years old, and were living in 8 Graham's Row, a two-room house

3   Edward Vaughan was born in December 1888, and having previously worked in Guinness's, he joined Jacob's in 1913 as employee number 1008. He worked in the engineering department and retired in January 1954, after forty-one years.

4   According to Jacob's archivist, Douglas Appleyard, Doyle may have been a timekeeper for the factory. 'Lost and found' items were typically handed in to the timekeepers' office, or to a manager.

close to Dorset Street, on Dublin's northside. James was a carpenter, and his oldest son's occupation is listed as 'apprentice to carpentry' – at this date, he's listed as 'Joseph Brown'.

By the 1911 census, Joseph was living half a mile away in 24 Synnott Place, a five-room house containing twenty-one people from eight families. Joseph was sharing a room with his younger brother John Patrick, and at this stage their name is recorded as Browne, with an e. However, we can see that the older Browne, as head of the household, has signed his name in Irish – Seosamh de Brúin.[5] Both brothers could speak Irish and both gave carpentry as their profession. By now a good number of the other Browne brothers had emigrated, many to America, where they became coach builders and stained glass merchants.

At some point before 1906, de Brún became a member of the Gaelic League, and on St Patrick's Day 1913 he was photographed along with another eighteen members of An Coiste Náisiúnta Tionsclaíochta (The National Industrial Committee).[6] This committee was responsible

5 Originally, de Brún signed his name as 'de Brúin', but later changed it to omit the 'i'. In a note included in his 1948 Army Pensions file, he wrote: 'I wish to correct an apparent misspelling of my name. In future I will sign Seosamh de Brún using the broad Gaelic vowel ú, instead of Seosamh de Brúin which is an early form of spelling the name, when Gaelic was not so generally established and its grammar so well understood.'

6 Now known as Conradh na Gaeilge, the Gaelic League was formed in 1893 to promote the Irish language. De Brún is mentioned in connection to League business in *The Freeman's Journal* several times before 1916, including 4 August 1906, 15 July 1908, 18 August 1909 and 28 January 1910.

The National Industrial Committee, St Patrick's Day, 1913.

Front (left to right): *Seán T. O'Kelly (also a member of the Gaelic League and Sinn Féin and an active Volunteer in the Rising; later a Dáil minister and President of Ireland); P. Ó hEithir; Pádraig Ó Dálaigh (Secretary-General of the Gaelic League and a member of the IRB); Liam Ó Maoláin (a member of the Gaelic League); Peadar Macken (a member of the IRB, very active in the Gaelic League, and an alderman in Dublin Corporation; he was accidentally killed at Boland's Mill during the Rising); Greg Murphy (a member of the Volunteers and possibly a participant in the Rising); G. Ó Grifín.*

Middle: *Michael O'Hanrahan (an IRB member and second-in-command of 2nd Battalion, Dublin Brigade; he fought under Commandant Thomas MacDonagh in Jacob's factory – the same garrison that de Brún fought with); Sean C. Ó Fearcheallaigh; SEOSAMH DE BRÚN; D. de Búrca (GAA Dublin Board Secretary); Cluad de Ceabhasa (or Claude Chavasse – an Englishman passionate about Irish culture); Henry O'Hanrahan (a member of the IRB and brother of Michael O'Hanrahan); N. Lennon (possibly Nicholas Lennon, listed as having fought in the Four Courts area in 1916); P. Mac an Aili; L. Ó Branagáin.*

Back: *Seosamh Mac Cionnaith (a member of the GAA); Seán M. O'Duffy (an active GAA member and camogie organiser – the senior camogie championship cup is named after him – he fought in the Four Courts area in 1916); Séamus Connolly (a member of the Gaelic League).*

Author's collection

for organising the St Patrick's Day parade and its aim was to encourage an industrial revival in Ireland and to help build up native Irish industries, and so the celebrations on St Patrick's Day took the form of an industrially themed parade.

All the men in the photo were members of the Gaelic League and/or the GAA (Chumann Lúthchleas Gael), but many were also members of the Irish Republican Brotherhood (IRB), and several went on to become well-known names in the struggle for Irish independence, including Seán T. O'Kelly and the O'Hanrahan brothers, Michael and Henry.

At least seven members of the committee fought in the Rising – one was executed, another killed accidentally – while Seán T. O'Kelly went on to be president of Ireland.

During 1914 a well-known Gaelic Leaguer, James J. Hughes (Seamus Ó hAodha),[7] was advocating an economic, industrial approach to the saving of Irish, 'urging the preservation of the Gaeltacht areas by economic development'.[8] In March 1914 Hughes announced that a special meeting had been arranged for Wynn's Hotel, Dublin, by a small group of Leaguers who had 'never been in the limelight' and were 'not identified with any party'. Among these was Seosamh de Brún.

People attended the meeting from all parts of the

7   Ó hAodha fought in Jacob's during the Rising.
8   Morrissey, Thomas, 'Saving the Language: "The Impatient Revolutionary"', in *Studies: An Irish Quarterly Review*, Vol. 77, No. 307 (Autumn, 1988), p. 352.

country. The proposed new strategy for the League seems to have found favour at the meeting, 'but, on the recommendation of Seosamh de Brún, they agreed to adjourn the meeting for three weeks lest their demand for a change of policy at that juncture might injure the language collection about to be inaugurated'.[9] However, this adjournment appears to have broken the impetus of the incipient movement and the proposal was never adopted by the League.

De Brún doesn't actually seem to have been one of the Gaelic Leaguers who fitted the description of never having 'been in the limelight' – on the contrary, he seems to have been a valued member of the League. In February 1915 *The Irish Times* reported that at a meeting of the League's Dublin Coiste Ceanntair, 'The financial report of the Collection Committee was adopted, and the meeting gave expression to the indebtedness of the Dublin League to the Hon. Secretary, Seosamh de Brún, for his work on behalf of the collection in 1913 and 1914.'

Despite this high praise, de Brún makes no mention of the Gaelic League in his 1916 diary, so it's possible that he left the organisation or, at the very least, took a less prominent role after 1914. His interest in the promotion of the language clearly didn't disappear though, because

9   Probably referring to the Gaelic League's *Seachtmhain na Gaedhilge* annual collection for the support of the language, held around St Patrick's Day – the Wynn's Hotel meeting was held on a date before 14 March. It would of course have been important not to jeopardise the success of the collection by announcing a possible change to the League's policy so close to the start of the collection.

in 1952 it was reported that Seosamh de Brún (then in his late sixties) was elected president of a newly formed branch of the League.[10]

But the Gaelic League wasn't the only organisation de Brún was involved with – as a carpenter, he was a member of the Amalgamated Society of Carpenters and Joiners, and, like his membership of other organisations, this union affiliation would have an impact on his life and is the subject of several entries in his diary.

On Sunday 2 April 1916, *The Irish Times* reported that 'The men of the Dublin building trade ceased work on Saturday.' Around 2,750 tradesmen and labourers had made demands for an increase in wages of between one and two pence per hour – employers had offered a halfpenny. The offer was refused and work was halted. De Brún seems to have been held in high regard in the union, because three days after the decision to strike, he writes: 'Elected to strike committee.' Unfortunately his poor financial situation worked against him and the next line reads: 'Debarred from sitting owing to arrears.' Not surprisingly de Brún is unimpressed with this particular union rule, and writes: 'Workers love liberty but a rule enslaves them.'

De Brún may also have been a member of the short-lived Socialist Party of Ireland (led by James Connolly) as in a deposition given in 1950 to the Bureau of Military History, Volunteer Thomas Pugh writes: 'I was very much on the Labour side in the 1913 strike. I joined the Socialist

10 *The Irish Press*, 1 March 1952.

Party of Ireland, of which James Connolly and William O'Brien were members ... William O'Brien's brother was a high up Volunteer officer. A man who lived in Ringsend was a member. He was a carpenter and I think his name was Browne. He was in Jacob's in Easter Week, 1916, with me.' Although de Brún didn't live in Ringsend until later in life (including the year 1950), as a carpenter with the name Browne, it seems very likely that he's the man Pugh is referring to.

Without a doubt, however, it was his membership of yet another organisation that was to have the greatest impact on de Brún's life – the Irish Volunteers. Formed in 1913, the Volunteers included many members of the Gaelic League (including several signatories of the Proclamation), so it's not surprising that de Brún joined the new movement at its very beginning, on 25 November at the Rotunda Rink. We can't say for sure what his position in the Volunteers was, but family history recounts that he was involved in the planning for the Easter Rising. What we do know for sure is that in 1916 de Brún was a member of 'B' Company, 2nd Battalion of the Dublin Brigade Irish Volunteers. From his diary we learn that he was company adjutant, at least for a time. Whatever rank he held in the Irish Volunteers, however, de Brún wrote about, and in some cases was present at, some of that organisation's defining moments in the run-up to the rebellion.

In January 1916 the houses of Countess Markievicz and four others were raided by the Dublin Metropolitan Police, causing the Volunteers to go on high alert. Then on 17 March, St Patrick's Day, 2,000 Irish Volunteers held what the *Sinn Féin Rebellion Handbook* called 'a field day in the city'. For two hours in the middle of the day, the armed men held up traffic around College Green while inspections were carried out, bands played and leaflets were distributed. The *Handbook* remarked that this was 'the first time the Irish Volunteers had taken aggressive action in daylight'.

Three days later Volunteers in Tullamore were engaged in more than manoeuvres when an anti-Sinn Féin crowd gathered outside the Volunteers' meeting hall. Stones were thrown and windows smashed, before a Volunteer inside fired shots. The police arrived and attempted to search the hall for arms, but more shots were fired and some policemen were injured. These are sometimes referred to as the first shots of the Easter Rising.[11]

Just days after that excitement, de Brún noted the seizure by the authorities of elements of what was known as the 'mosquito press'. *The Spark, Honesty, The Gael* and *The Gaelic Athlete* were being shut down – all newspapers which published anti-British propaganda. A warrant had been issued by Major General Friend with the order to seize and remove not just any printed papers 'likely to cause disaffection to His Majesty, The King', but the

11 A more widely accepted claim for the first shot of the Rising was made by the Laois Volunteers, who apparently fired it after destroying a section of railway track at a place called Colt Wood on the night of 23 April – the day before the Rising began in Dublin. See O'Farrell, M., *50 Things You Didn't Know About 1916*, pp. 20–1.

presses they had been printed on.[12] The machinery of Joe Stanley's Gaelic Press was dismantled and lorries removed it to Dublin Castle.

On Monday 27 March three prominent organisers for the Irish Volunteers, Ernest Blythe, Liam Mellows and Alfred Monaghan, were served with deportation orders relating to their activities, which the authorities regarded as 'endeavouring to prejudice recruiting or the public safety'.[13] A protest meeting was held at Dublin's Mansion House on 30 March, but despite speeches inside 'of a strong character', it was what happened later outside that really made headlines.[14] A crowd of people who had attended the meeting gathered outside, traffic was blocked and shots were fired. 'Voltrs ready for immediate action', wrote de Brún.

Closer to the start of the rebellion, on 19 April, de Brún notes: 'Corporation meeting. Kellys speech & documents re preparations against Volunteers. Our fellows seething with "nerves".' This was the meeting at which Alderman Tom Kelly famously read into the record the contents of what has become known as the Castle Document – a list of apparently imminent arrests, including leaders of Sinn Féin, the Volunteers and the Gaelic League. Reaction to this document ranged from disbelief to outrage and,

12 Reilly, Tom, *Joe Stanley: Printer to the Rising*, Brandon, Dingle, 2005, p. 28.
13 Royal Commission on the Rebellion in Ireland, *Minutes of Evidence and Appendix of Documents*, HMSO, London, 1916, p. 5.
14 *The Irish Times*, Friday 31 March 1916.

regardless of its authenticity, it is credited by some as having played a significant part in the actions which led to the Rising itself.

Meanwhile, de Brún's position in the Volunteer ranks doesn't seem to have been a happy one, and shortly before the publication of the Castle Document, on 11 April, he writes: 'B. Coy. Coldness. The limit reached. Left early. Considered resignation.' It seems he didn't need to take long to consider it, because on 15 April he writes: 'Handed Hunter & O'Reilly my resignation ...'[15] And on 18 April: 'Met O'Connor. Gave him copy of resignation of adjutancy.'[16]

Nevertheless, de Brún remained with the Volunteers, and in between diary entries on the carpenters' strike and the Volunteers' activities, de Brún recorded the tension and air of expectation immediately preceding the actual outbreak of the rebellion on 24 April, in spite of the secrecy surrounding it. On 23 April: 'Excitement intense.

15 Thomas Hunter was an officer with the 2nd Battalion – he is referred to by various sources as commandant, vice-commandant or captain. Volunteer William James Stapleton, who also served in Jacob's in 1916 with 'B' Company, 2nd Battalion, recalled later that when he joined in 1915: 'Tom Hunter was my Company Captain or Organiser at the time. Another officer was a man called O'Reilly.' During the Rising itself, de Brún refers to Hunter as commandant. Frank Henderson, in his memoirs, wrote that 'The Captain of "B" Company was Peadar O'Reilly, who was a delicate man. We got word on Saturday that he got a haemorrhage of the lungs, and ... was brought to the Mater Hospital.' From Hopkinson, M. (ed.), *Frank Henderson's Easter Rising*, p. 39.

16 When applying for a pension under the Military Service Pensions Act 1934, de Brún gave his rank as 'Adjutant B Coy, 2nd Batt' and said he'd been appointed to the position 'About the end of 1914'. He didn't make any reference to his resignation.

The crisis is near.' The next day, the Easter Rising began and de Brún, apparently as a rank and file Volunteer, didn't hesitate to take part.

As well as his active membership of these organisations, de Brún's diary also records events in his personal life. Unfortunately for him, the main subject is employment and money, and at the end of 1915 the year ahead didn't seem to hold many prospects. At the very start of the diary, de Brún writes: '1915. Before Christmas. Resolution to "Economise" by putting smoking + drinking alcohol to one side at least until I pull business round a bit and clear of debt.' It appears, however, that de Brún may have still allowed himself one vice – written at the back of the diary are the names of various soccer teams, along with betting odds and sums of money!

On various other dates he writes: 'Blue prospects', 'Troubles multiplying', 'Business very dull', 'No money for Digs'. De Brún's trade was carpentry, and in 1916 he had his own business of 'Joseph Browne – Carpenter and Contractor', operating out of No. 9 Lower Exchange Street.[17] However, the only work he mentions throughout the diary is the construction of wooden cases to carry artillery shells to the guns on the war front in France and, although he may have been involved in negotiating the price per case, it is not clear whether he was actually doing any of the work himself.

17 De Brún appears as 'Browne, J., contractor' at 9 Lower Exchange Street in *Thom's Official Directory* for 1916 and 1917.

As mentioned previously, it appears that his financial troubles prevented him from being appointed to the carpenters' strike committee in April 1916. Throughout the year there seems to be a substantially larger sum of money going out than coming in and in mid-April de Brún wrote: 'If not hanged or drowned I will be strangled with debt.' Nevertheless, despite the temptation of regular paid work in England – 'It would pay me to go to Gretna, & most people put their own personal interests first in their actions' – de Brún stayed in Ireland. (Interestingly, family history includes a story that de Brún inherited £2,000 in the early 1900s from an uncle in Meath, and that he used it for, or gave it towards, the purchase of guns. There's also a family rumour that he played a part in the Howth gun-running, which is entirely possible, since other Volunteers' accounts confirm that members of 'B' Company, 2nd Battalion took part.)[18]

There are other aspects of de Brún's personal life referred to throughout the diary's pages – aspects that clearly had a major influence on him. These are, in many ways, very ordinary, and could reasonably be said to have had no bearing on anything de Brún did for the cause of the Gaelic League, the carpenters' union, or even the Irish Volunteers. But they impacted on him as a person, and so could just as reasonably be said to have played a part in influencing everything he did. Whatever the reality of it, it's the ordinariness of these personal, sometimes short,

18 For example, Pádraig Ó Ceallaigh, BMH WS 376, p. 1.

sometimes cryptic notes, written in between historic events, that illustrate perfectly the ordinariness of the individual who wrote them. Seosamh de Brún was an ordinary man who got caught up in extraordinary events in 1916, just like Samuel Henry Lomas and all the other ordinary men who found themselves on a similar path, on both sides of the rebellion.[19]

The diary's year is only three days old when de Brún writes: 'Visited by Mrs Fegan & Mrs Hoey Re A. Walshe.' Mrs Hoey is mentioned twice more, and 'A. Walshe' has eight more entries, sometimes without the final 'e', and other times as simply 'A.W.' Mrs Frances Hoey (neé Walsh) was married to a gardener on the Powerscourt estate, and worked in the kitchens of Powerscourt House. 'A. Walshe' was Ann Walsh, Mrs Hoey's sister, and the mother of de Brún's daughter Agnes, born on 30 December 1915, just four days earlier.[20] Mrs Hoey's companion on the visit was Mrs Fegan, a relative of hers and Ann's, possibly an aunt. We don't know how old de Brún's relationship with Ann Walsh was, but we do know that they weren't married and so the birth of a child would have brought with it many complications.

From subsequent entries, we can see that de Brún visits Ann (or Annie) a few times, and there are sums of money mentioned. However, Agnes is never referred to, and after 16 April there are no more mentions of Ann.

---

19 See *Absolutely full of Sinn Féinners*, p. 155.
20 Information provided by Una Byrne O'Carroll, Agnes Browne's daughter, and Seosamh de Brún's granddaughter.

Shortly after that last reference, and despite the building tension in the city, the outbreak of the Rising on Easter Monday came as a surprise to de Brún, who 'did not expect to be engaged in Revolution, at least so suddenly'. And it is tempting to think that, finding himself in the middle of a rebellion, he may have welcomed the chance to throw himself into an enterprise where money and personal worries would be the last things on his mind. Certainly there's a marked change in the tone which comes across when he's making notes during the Rising: 'I review my life. I believe I was fated to be here today. I could not have escaped it.'

The diary's final reference to de Brún's private life is on the morning of the Rising when, before he hears of the mobilisation, he was 'Going to Scalp with Mattie'.

Mattie (Martha) Maguire was the woman who de Brún later married, but on 24 April she was due to go with him to the Scalp, a narrow wooded valley south of Dublin city popular with day-trippers at the time. However, the trip was immediately cancelled when de Brún noticed some Volunteers hurrying for an emergency mobilisation – the rebellion was actually happening, despite the last-minute cancellation of manoeuvres caused by Eoin MacNeill's countermanding orders of the day before. MacNeill had failed to halt the Rising and had merely delayed it by a day.

De Brún quickly found himself in action – 'excited and hurried movements'. The 2nd Battalion of the Volunteers was tasked with occupying and holding the huge bulk of Jacob's biscuit factory and its surroundings. 'We are in action, boys,' proclaimed Captain Tom Hunter, and de Brún wrote: 'We know fight & die [sic] is necessary for a free Irish Republic.'

Nearby streets and some smaller buildings were occupied, and some barricades constructed. The reaction of the locals was mixed, and while some were merely curious, many were hostile. While in the Blackpitts area, de Brún wrote: 'Populace don't understand', and attempts were made to tear down the barricades. Some even fought among themselves, and de Brún, filled as he was with the excitement and tension of action, wrote angrily: 'Are these the people we are trying to free? Are they worth fighting for? The dregs of the population', before calming himself: 'Patience!' Prophetically he added: 'Tomorrow they will cheer us.' De Brún was relieved when recalled to the main Jacob's building, although he described it as vast and dark.

The next day, Tuesday, was spent fortifying the Volunteers' position, and there was a bit more time for reflection and indeed, for the reality of the situation to sink in. De Brún reiterated his surprise: 'I was annoyed at mobilisation yesterday. It spoiled my anticipated day's outing. But "man proposes" etc.'[21] However, the men soon started to settle into their situation: 'We believe we are going to make a sacrifice. We offer it to god & our country.' A flow of information was coming into the garrison, relating news of the rebellion in other parts of the city and

21 The full proverb is 'Man proposes, God disposes'.

around the country: 'Keeps up our spirits.' Nevertheless, one Volunteer hadn't fully come to terms with being a sudden revolutionary. Paddy Callan, a fellow carpenter, was nervous, wrote de Brún, adding of him: 'Can't sleep & bad digestion.'

Thankfully the situation had improved for Callan by the next day: 'Paddy Callan is quite calm today. Poor Pat. Like me he did not expect to be engaged in Revolution at least so suddenly.' In fact, the men in Jacob's probably saw the least military action of all the rebel garrisons. With its imposing bulk, the factory was an excellent position from a defensive point of view, and if the military had wanted to take it by a direct assault, it would have come at the cost of a great number of lives. For the moment, however, the British took the decision to more or less bypass the rebels holed up inside the factory walls and by Wednesday, when artillery was in action on Sackville Street and terrible struggles were taking place at Mount Street Bridge and the Mendicity Institution, life within the walls of Jacob's was arguably becoming more relaxed.

De Brún writes of 'fun & good spirits' and says: 'Provisioning here is perfect – tons of flour, sugar, & biscuits and those girls working so hard.'[22] The small number of Cumann na mBan women present in the factory were greatly appreciated: 'Only in great moments like those

---

22 Volunteer Thomas Pugh, a fellow member of 'B' Company, recalled that they 'found a lot of crystallised fruit and tons of chocolate at the top of the house and we gorged ourselves. We were well off as regards that kind of food, but we would have given a lot for an ordinary piece of bread.'

does one get a *true* glimpse of Womanhood, patient self-sacrificing & cheerfully brave.'[23]

The factory's location was so quiet that at least one priest was able to enter the building and take confessions from some of the men, including de Brún – 'I have been to confession. First time for years. I feel better for it.'[24] Religion, and specifically Catholicism, was a very important part of many of the rebels' lives, and for de Brún, it was inseparable from Ireland and Irishness. 'I do believe that the Catholic Religion and Irish nationality are ... so interwoven. The spirit of Christ & Irish Nationality. The spirit of progress & sacrifice.'

That Wednesday night, the Volunteers expected an attack – 'Men of our section nervous, officers also apprehensive. 1 A.M. new barricades finished jaded tired. Sleep in equipment.' Nevertheless, Thursday arrived without an overnight assault.

Although Jacob's wasn't subjected to attack, some of the men were active in other ways – the factory towers provided excellent lookout posts, as well as sniper nests. Rebel snipers were able to harass not just the military in nearby streets,

---

23 There were only six Cumann na mBan women in the garrison, according to the leader of the group, Máire Nic Shiubhlaigh, in *The Splendid Years*, her book of recollections. Volunteer John MacDonagh recalled that 'everyone of them was prepared to give her life'. In addition, Volunteer Seamus Pounch noted that there were some Clan na Gael Girl Scouts 'represented by Capt. May Kelly, who formed part of the garrison'.

24 In his memoirs, Peadar Kearney wrote of Jacob's that 'inside, Rev Father Metcalfe, O.C.C., spent the week doing all he could to prepare men for death' – de Burca, Seamus, *The Soldier's Song: The story of Peadar Kearney*, P.J. Bourke, Dublin, 1957.

but also soldiers in the Rathmines Barracks and as far off as the St Stephen's Green area. De Brún was put on watch duty till 1 p.m. on Thursday, and by now the sounds of warfare seemed much closer and louder: 'Darkness & silence save for the rattle of rifles & machine guns.' He writes that he 'expected to be riddled, though inside building', and when his guard shift was over he admits to feeling 'highly strung, can't sleep expecting attack'.

Friday arrived and still the garrison were generally at ease: 'resting at base on luxurious improvised settees ... The boys discussing the ... revolution.' With the local situation still so quiet after five days of occupation, it must have seemed to the rank and file Volunteers that the rebellion was going well across the city, and maybe even the country.[25] 'May the Republic endure, Ireland will endure. Freedom has been asserted', wrote de Brún.

Saturday, however, brought not just a change in atmosphere, but a literal change of scenery.

John O'Grady, seen here with the bicycle he was riding when he was fatally wounded.
Courtesy of Séan and Caroline Brady (with thanks to Ray Bateson)

25 Kearney wrote that 'so far as the rank and file in Jacob's was concerned, there was absolutely no authentic news as to what was taking place elsewhere.'

An artist's impression of Jacob's factory around the time of the Rising.
Bishop Street is to the left, and Peter Row to the right. It's easy to see why
the factory's buildings gave rebel snipers clear views over the city – it's also

easy to see why Volunteer Callan was worried about the big chimney crashing down. Author's collection

De Brún was 'called early & selected to form a "Diverting Party"' of armed cyclists who were to cycle towards the Boland's Mill and Mount Street area, with a view to relieving the pressure on Éamon de Valera's garrison.[26] Fourteen men left Jacob's and made their way around Merrion Square, via Leeson Street, almost as far as Holles Street. Here, de Brún writes: 'Dismount opened fire remount return.'

On the return journey, British army snipers opened fire as the cyclists were turning back into York Street and, while running a 'gauntlet of shots', one of the men was hit: 'O'Grady shot here.' John O'Grady was helped back to the factory, from where he was brought to the Adelaide Hospital, which at that time was across Peter Street from Jacob's. This bicycle sortie was the most important action the Jacob's garrison were involved in, and it must have been a frightening experience – de Brún writes of himself: 'I did not think I would return.'

O'Grady subsequently died, but de Brún couldn't have known that when he was writing in his diary, which would explain the apparent casualness of his next entry: 'Easy day. Read portion of "Julius Caesar".' Jacob's was considered a progressive employer, and among the advantages its employees enjoyed was a library, which was broken into by the rebels and its contents read and studied during off-duty hours.

De Brún's final lines in the diary are about his opinion of the reconciliation in Shakespeare's play, *Julius Caesar*,

26 See *A Sortie from Jacob's*, p. 134.

between Marcus Brutus and Gaius Cassius – he calls it 'an ideal conception of the idea of the Brotherhood of man and free from cant or cheap political platitude.'[27] Given the circumstances in which he was writing this, it may seem incongruous that he was spending time analysing Shakespeare, but given also what we know about de Brún's difficult year up until then – union difficulties, Volunteer activities, etc. – it's interesting to get a glimpse into his thoughts as the Rising was coming to an end, and easy to see why the concept of an ideal 'Brotherhood of man' would be attractive.

Of course, the fact that, as the fighting in other rebel garrisons was coming to its violent, deadly end, a member of the Jacob's garrison was able to take the time to read Shakespeare and write comments on it, speaks volumes about the military situation in and around the factory.[28] De Brún's notes on *Caesar* were probably written on the evening of the Saturday, and they were the last words he entered in the diary. By then the GPO was ablaze and abandoned, and the rebel leaders, surrounded in Moore Street, had actually surrendered, as had the Four Courts garrison.

27 Brutus and Cassius were co-conspirators in the assassination of Julius Caesar. The two fell out afterwards, but were reconciled before a battle with Caesar's supporters, in which they both died.
28 Volunteer Thomas Pugh wrote later: 'The only time I was in the firing was when I was on the top floor of Jacobs, where they had a rest-room and library, with a glass roof and glass windows. A bullet came through ... I was mostly on the ground floor and only went up to the library to look for a book' (BMH WS 397, pp. 5–6).

News of the rebellion's collapse came to Jacob's on Sunday morning, and after speeches from their leaders, most of the garrison marched out to surrender, while some merged into the crowd that had gathered outside and escaped.[29] De Brún was one of those who escaped and consequently his name doesn't appear on any prisoner lists. His small diary, in which he had recorded history as it happened, was left behind to be discovered by Edward Vaughan.

What de Brún did in the aftermath of the Rising isn't clear – family history relates that he was on the run, yet he was openly operating out of 9 Lower Exchange Street for possibly another eighteen months. Indeed, some of his original invoices still survive, including one from mid-July 1916, not long after the rebellion ended. De Brún was 'supplying and fitting' slates on the roof of a commercial premises in Capel Street, and it's not impossible that he was repairing damage caused during the rebellion. Then, in the 1918 edition of *Thom's Directory*, de Brún is no longer listed at No. 9, and in his application for a military pension, he states that he 'got a dose of 'flue [sic] in 1918'.[30]

De Brún's Service Certificate, prepared in relation to his application for a Military Service Pension in 1937, states that he rendered service with the Irish Volunteers for the 'entire period' between 23 April 1916 and 31 March 1919. However, when he applied for a Service (1917–1921)

29 See *Escape from Jacob's*, p. 146.
30 The 1918 influenza pandemic infected 500 million people worldwide, and killed between 50 and 100 million.

Medal in 1944 he was unsuccessful, despite stating that he was a member of the Irish Volunteers and Irish Republican Army from 1913–1922, and was 'always on reserve'. Under the heading 'nature of service' he wrote: 'Reorganisation of IRA; Supporting dependants of interned members; Political assistance Sinn Fein party; Availability for service in IRA when called on.' (In answer to the question 'Address at which you resided on 11th July 1921', de Brún entered '14 Mornington Road, Liverpool.')

Two witness statements contradicted these statements. Firstly, in an undated note, Tommy Clarke 'Late Adjt, B Coy, 2nd Batt, Dublin Brigade, Old IRA' wrote: 'As far as I can remember this man left Ireland about the end of 1916 or early in 1917 and to my knowledge did not report back to his Unit before the Truce. On these grounds I cannot recommend him for a Service Medal.' Then, a report signed by Joseph N. Troy, 'Hon Sec Batt', on behalf of F. Henderson, Commandant, states that de Brún 'was out for the 1916 week only', and adds: 'All the men of B Coy Batt II now available are definite that this man did not attend the Coy at any time between 1916 and 1921. Not entitled to General Service Medal.' In contrast another, undated, illuminated certificate states that Joseph Browne fought for the freedom of Ireland from 1916 to 1921, and is signed by, among others, Oscar Traynor.

By October 1935 Volunteer de Brún was living in Ireland and was invited by the Easter Week Memorial Committee to sign the Easter Week Roll of Honour – a document which was intended to be 'a complete Roll of the surviving participants in the Easter Week Rising, 1916'. This was to be 'lodged in the National Museum as a National document' and in 1936 the Roll of Honour was presented to the government.

During the Second World War, de Brún was back in uniform in his mid-50s, as a member of the 26th Battalion, which was composed of veterans of the War of Independence. From his military pension files we learn that de Brún served in the Maintenance Department of the Army Corps of Engineers as a carpenter from 1940 to 1958 – forty-two years after he fought in 1916.

We also know that, despite the setback he experienced in 1916 during the carpenters' strike, de Brún remained a committed and active member of the carpenters' union throughout his life. In 1921 the Amalgamated Society of Carpenters and Joiners merged with the General Union of Carpenters and Joiners, to form the Amalgamated Society of Woodworkers. And when de Brún was elected president of a new Gaelic League branch in 1952, he was part of a branch formed within the Amalgamated Society of Woodworkers.

De Brún also served his fellow Dubliners as a Labour member of Dublin Corporation for at least one term in the mid-1940s.

Mattie Maguire also remained part of de Brún's life, and the two were married on 30 September 1920, eventually living in Irishtown in Dublin. Meanwhile, Ann Walsh left for America soon after Agnes was born. The child was raised by her aunt, Frances Hoey, and, for some time at

*Seosamh de Brún with his medals on Easter Monday, 11 April 1966.
Photographed outside his house in Irishtown with his grandson, Sean Ó
Broin, on the way to the GPO for the Golden Jubilee commemorations
of the 1916 Rising (note the Tricolour attached to the car), Seosamh's
family later took him to the Cappagh House pub in Finglas, which
was holding a special event for the occasion. There he was welcomed up
on stage as the band played* A Nation Once Again *and the national
anthem,* Amhrán na bhFiann, *which, by all accounts Seosamh sang
with great gusto. The medals (left to right), are the 1916 medal, the
Emergency medal for service in the 26th Battalion during WWII (which
has two bars, awarded for service over the qualifying period), and the
1966 anniversary medal.*
Courtesy of Una Byrne O'Carroll

least, de Brún sent money to Ann in America. In time, Agnes Browne reared four boys and two girls of her own. 'Grandfather Joe' would visit at times, and he helped the carpentry trade to continue in the family by organising for three of his grandsons to become carpenters.

In 1965 de Brún applied for a Special Allowance under the Army Pensions Act, and among the documents he was required to supply was a medical certificate from the Dublin Board of Assistance, which stated that, among other ailments, the applicant was suffering from deafness, arthritis and cataracts, and was 'permanently incapable of self-support'.

Seosamh de Brún died on 2 September 1968 and received a funeral with military honours. The Tricolour that draped his coffin was presented to his wife Mattie, who died a few years later, in the 1970s. Seosamh and Ann Walsh's daughter, Agnes Browne, died on 21 November 1990.

Transcript of the 1916 Diary of Volunteer Seosamh de Brún[1]

Written inside the front cover:

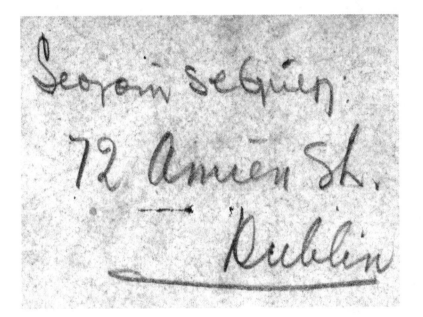

<hr />

1   Initially, comparison of the day-by-day entries with the images of the actual diary may be confusing. This is because de Brún sometimes needed more than the allotted day's space in the diary to record all his thoughts, so he simply continued to write over subsequent pages, regardless of the date. Then, when beginning the next day's entry, he would write the day and date onto the page himself.

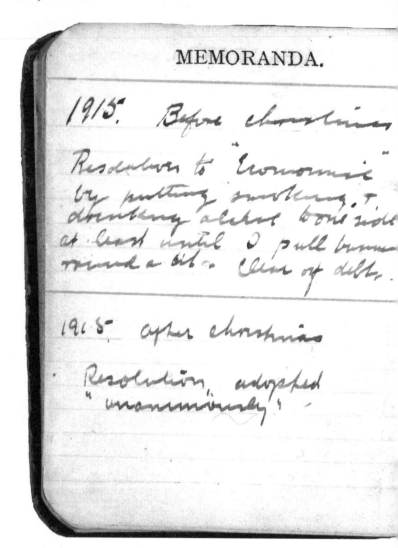

MEMORANDA.

1915. Before christmas

Resolution to "Economise" by putting smoking, + drinking alcohol to one side at least until I pull business round a bit & Clear of debts,

1915. after christmas

Resolution, adopted "unanimously" —

1915. Before Christmas

Resolution to 'Economise' by putting smoking + drinking alcohol to one side at least until I pull business round a bit and clear of debts.

JANUARY, 1916.

Saturday 1

Blue prospects for coming year. Expect troublous times, & bad employment, as *[illegible]* may have to close down no 9, Slacking power, in business may. easy mid to speak of.

Sunday 2

2nd after Christmas

"avoiding the occasion of sin" & The releasing Atmosphere of the Public use "No dull beginning

1915. After Christmas

Resolution adopted 'unanimously'

JANUARY, 1916

Saturday 1

Blue prospects for coming year. Expect troubling times & bad employment in Ireland, may have to close down no 9. __ in business may __! Nice to speak of.[2]

Sunday 2

Avoiding 'the occasion of sin'. The relaxing atmosphere of the Public House. It's [a] dull beginning.

Monday 3

Visited by Miss Fagan[3] & Miss Hoey Re A. Walshe.

Visited by Michael – 'Money or your life'?[4]

Tuesday 4

England. Plenty of work & good wages there.

6 months would 'free' me from debt & perhaps enable me to 'carry on' business again.

Wednesday 5

Troubles multiplying! It's a damn good job I adopted resolution of 1915 otherwise I might be inclined to seek solace in creamy pints & maudlin sentiment. A clear head will carry me through

2 Where words could not be deciphered this has been indicated with __.

3 De Brún seems to have written 'Fagan', although her name was Fegan. See p. 32 on Fegan, Hoey and Walshe.

4 Possibly refers to de Brún's brother Michael, six years his junior.

JANUARY, 1916.

Monday 3

Visited by Mrs Fagan & Mrs Hoey
Re a. Walshe.

Visited by Michael —
" Money or your life" ?

Tuesday 4

England. Plenty of work
& food wages there,
6 months would 'free' me
from debt & perhaps
enable me to "carry on"
business again

with that fortitude which I never lacked.

1916 will be a trial year

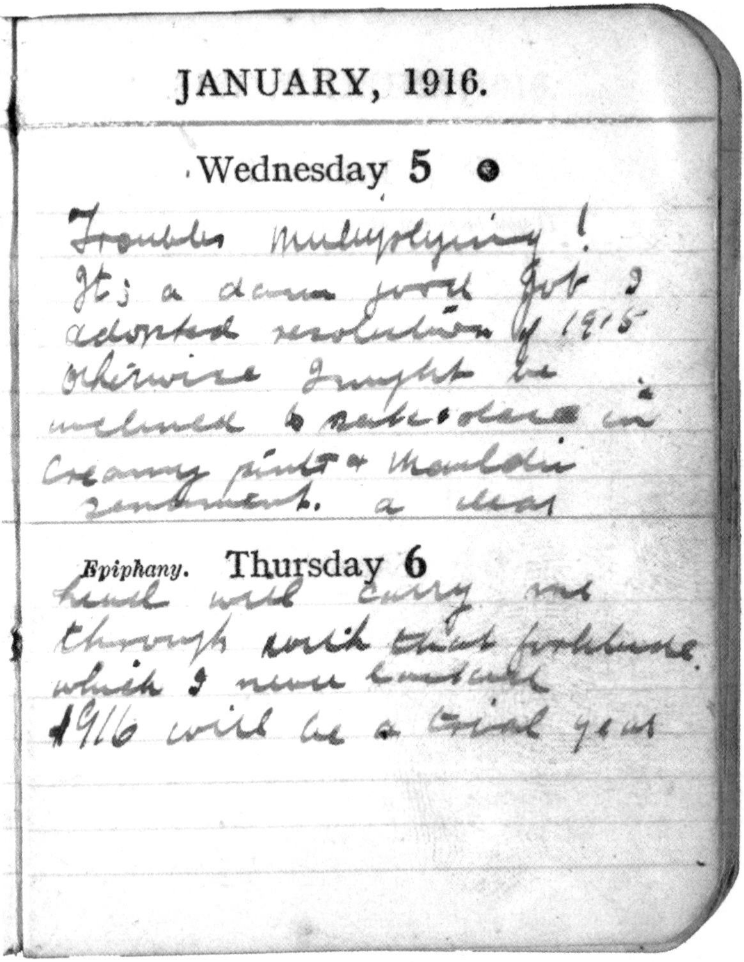

JANUARY, 1916.

Wednesday 5

Troubles multiplying! It's a damn good job I adopted resolution of 1915 otherwise I might be inclined to subside in creamy pints & maudlin sentiment. A clear

Epiphany. Thursday 6

head will carry me through with that fortitude which I never lacked

1916 will be a trial year

Monday 17

Visited A.W.

Tuesday 18

Looking for 'Securities'.

A man would lay down his life for a 'principal' — if there was no 'interest' attached to it. It is easy to obtain salvation. It is damn hard to get money.

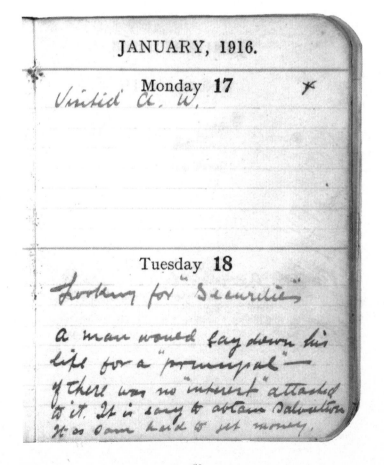

Thursday 20

Visited A. Walsh.

Friday 21

Visited Mrs Hoey.

Saturday 22

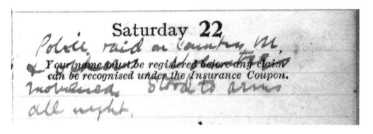

Police raid on Countess M. & others. Volunteers involved. Stood to arms all night.[5]

Monday 24

Business very dull. Good in England, which is to __

5   *The Irish Times* of 28 January 1916 reported that 'the house in Dublin of Countess Markievicz was searched by the Dublin Metropolitan Police … under a warrant issued by the Officer Commanding the Troops in Dublin. A printing press and a number of leaflets of an anti-British character were seized. No arrests were made.' The paper goes on to note that four other houses were searched on the same date and 'a few rifles were seized'. On this occasion, as on others, the Volunteers would have turned out in a show of force, the aim of which was not only to protect premises from further raids, but also to taunt the authorities.

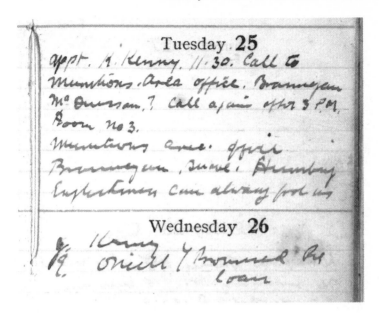

Tuesday 25

Appt. K. Kenny. 11.30. Call to Munitions Area office.[6] Branne-gan. McQussan. ? Call again after 3 P.M.

Room No 3.

Munitions Area office

Brannegan suave. Humbug Englishness can alway [*sic*] fool us

Wednesday 26

J. Kenny
E. O'Neill
} Promised Re loan

---

6   This seems to be in relation to setting a price to be paid per box for the
    wooden artillery shell cases that carpenters (and members of de Brún's
    union) were making to carry ammunition to the war front.

Friday 28 (

Letter from Delaney to F McCormack re munitions box to examine.

Price 5/- each. Dublin joinery mnftrs[7] are soldiers [?] for the government.

Saturday 29

Appt A. Walsh. Didn't go, proposed arrangement upset by Miss H visit to my Brother.[8]

Monday 31

Est. munitions boxes 4/-

7   Appears to be shorthand for 'manufacturers'.
8   De Brún had six younger brothers: James Francis, John Pat, Michael, William, Anthony and Edward.

FEBRUARY, 1916

Friday 11

Call A. Walshe 5 p.m.

Saturday 12

A.W. £2.2.0

Sunday 13

Would go to England but for Michael[9]

Monday 14

Society 7/6[10]

Monday 21

Attend S.F. soc[11]

John + Michael,[12] O'Neill, ___

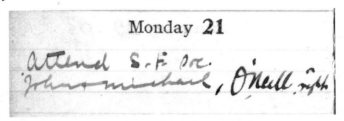

9   Another possible reference to his brother Michael.
10 It's unclear what society this refers to. It could be de Brún's union, the Amalgamated Society of Carpenters and Joiners. However, seven weeks later, on 3 April, he seems to be in arrears with the union, so this entry could refer to the 'Sinn Féin society' (see following note).
11 S.F. most likely stands for Sinn Féin.
12 Possible reference to two of de Brún's brothers.

FEBRUARY, 1916.

Thursday 24

Broken. securely for. him [25]

Friday 25

. Broken, Visit from Financial
a Jew, a big a fat. so no personal
are you married? no! good day
nothing doing. Whats the
use of robbing unconscious people
of no property, It is poor sport & most
unchristian. all experience is against
in favour of fleecing married people
whatever they possess, if a man has

property & nature is his work possessor property
is the standard lost of honesty. & it is far
more pious & anti legal to run a home
than to punish a debtor by other means

FEBRUARY, 1916.

Saturday 26

Sexa-gesima. Sunday 27

Carpenters meeting &
increase of wages
Volunteers progress
would like brie broth
through. But it "would"
pay me better to go to
England

B

59

Wednesday 23

R^{c.} cheque £26-14-6 E. Postage 2

Paid Michael £25-0-0

Thursday 24

Bracken. Security for. him £5-

Friday 25

Bracken. Visit from 'Financier' a Jew, a big ___. Some remarks[:] are you married? No! good day nothing doing. What's the use of robbing ~~single~~ unmarried people of no property. It is poor sport and most unchristian. All experience is ___ & in favour of fleecing married people of whatever they possess. If a man has no 'property' what use is his word. Possession of property is the standard test of honesty. It is far more pious & quite legal to ruin a home than to punish a debtor by other means.[13]

Sunday 27

Carpenters meeting re increase of wages

Volunteers progress[:] would like to see both through. But it 'would' pay me better to go to England[14]

---

13 It's unclear whether de Brún is describing an attempt to borrow money, or an attempt to talk terms on money he already owes. Either way, the negotiations aren't going his way.

14 The lure of dependable paid work in England is a constant temptation for de Brún, despite his personal ties to Ireland and his active involvement with various nationalist organisations.

MARCH, 1916

Thursday 9

Job in Gretna, circular received from Labor Exchange.[15]

Shall I go & wait over for carpenters trade movement?

It would pay me to go to Gretna, & most people put their own personal interests first in their actions.

15 His Majesty's Factory, Gretna, was an enormous explosives factory built in response to a dangerous shortage of munitions which developed in 1915. Construction began in November 1915 and production of munitions began in April 1916. Whole villages were custom built, with their own utilities, services and infrastructure. The entire complex spanned twelve miles, and would have required huge numbers of construction workers. Given the numbers of men joining the armed forces, it's not surprising that tradesmen were actively sought in Ireland.

Saturday 11

A.W. 12/-

Friday 17 (St Patrick's Day)

Vol^trs College Green (1st) Parade.[16]

Saturday 18

Bank a/c closed

Business 'at ease'

16 Three years earlier, de Brún was a member of the committee responsible for organising the 1913 St Patrick's Day parade to encourage an industrial revival in Ireland. In 1916 he is with the Volunteers and the parade had a much different purpose – a martial display, both of intent and of strength. There were around 2,000 participants in a parade of the battalions and companies of the Irish Volunteers and the Citizen Army – it was reported as 'the first time the Irish Volunteers had taken aggressive action in daylight'. The event began with mass in SS Michael and John's church, Lower Exchange Street (the same street where de Brún operated his contractor business), after which the Volunteers marched to College Green. There according to Seán Cody, they 'held that portion of Dame St. from the City Hall to the Bank of Ireland for over an hour, during which time no traffic was allowed to break the ranks …' (BMH WS 1035, p. 6). Bicycle-mounted Volunteers closed College Green to traffic, while Chief of Staff Eoin MacNeill reviewed the marchers. At one point, recalled Volunteer John J. Keegan, a motor car carrying the Commander-in-Chief of the British forces in Ireland, Major General Friend, attempted to drive through the cyclists, but was forced to turn back by Lieutenant Malone of the 3rd Battalion Volunteers, later to be killed in action at Mount Street Bridge (BMH WS 217, p. 23). The parade was important to the way the Volunteers were seen by the authorities, and by themselves, as there was a growing feeling among them that rebellion was afoot. According to Cumann na mBan member Margaret Kennedy, 'we were under orders to be ready as this might be the "real thing", meaning, of course, the Rising. We all wore full equipment and carried rations for twelve hours' (BMH WS 185, p. 2). Volunteer Seán Murphy wrote that St Patrick's Day was one of 'four tentative dates arranged for the actual rising' (BMH WS 204, p. 2), while Volunteer Seamus Grace was actually told to expect the rising to start that day (BMH WS 310, p. 3).

Monday 20

Tullamore police + Vol[trs] in action.[17] 9 casualties among police

17 In Tullamore, County Offaly, on the evening of Monday 20 March, what
    The Irish Times of 22 March referred to as 'ill-feeling which had been
    smouldering in the town for some time against the Sinn Féin Volunteers'
    finally boiled over. A small number of Volunteers and Cumann na mBan
    were in the Sinn Féin Hall on William Street when a hostile crowd
    gathered outside – 'mostly wives and hangers-on of the British Army',
    according to Volunteer Captain Peadar Bracken (BMH WS 361, p. 4).
    The Cumann na mBan women were escorted home by Bracken and
    Volunteer Joe Wrafter, and shortly after the two men returned, events
    turned violent. According to the *Sinn Féin Rebellion Handbook*, 'a number
    of children carrying a Union Jack sang songs ... the crowd soon swelled,
    and amid booing and cheering stone-throwing began, and the windows
    of the hall were smashed.' Bracken fired a couple of shots and soon the
    Royal Irish Constabulary arrived in force, demanding to be allowed
    to search the hall for arms. The Volunteers refused, more shots were
    fired and fighting began with sticks and batons. Despite being struck
    several times, Bracken escaped through the mob and evaded capture.
    Twelve others were eventually arrested and charged with offences
    including attempted murder, endangering 'the safety of His Majesty's
    forces' (Sergeant Ahern was shot more than once and seriously injured),
    'attempting to cause disaffection among the civilian population' and
    possessing 'certain documents likely to cause disaffection to his Majesty'
    (BMH WS 49). The reaction in Dublin was mixed. Volunteer Feargus de
    Burca was in P. H. Pearse's school, St Enda's, when 'word came through
    ... that the first shot of the Insurrection had been fired in Tullamore',

I serious, arrests, 1st blood drawn suggests we ___ on 'hell'
The weathers [?] cold anyway.

Thursday 23

Seizure of 'Spark' 'Honesty' 'Gael' & printing machinery taken to castle, military & police armed.[18] 1st appearance of military. Soldiering is an interesting occupation. It is not more dangerous than repairing houses, no worry by tailors or 'touching' friends, I believe I am developing the martial instinct.

Sunday 26

Meeting of Carpenters. Proposed strike Resolution. Composed by McParltin [sic],[19] it coincided with my views only 2 dissentients. I believe I am qualifying to become a 'Labor advocate' a paying profession.

adding that 'the place resounded with our cheers when P. H. Pearse announced the tidings to us' (BMH WS 694, p. 4). And while it would seem that Pearse was happy to pass on the cheerful news, other leaders were not so impressed. Charles Wyse-Power described the 'clash' in Tullamore in uncomplimentary terms: 'As a result of a police attack on them some of the Volunteers lost their tempers and fired on the police ... to the great annoyance of Tom Clarke and Seán McDermott' (BMH WS 420, p. 11). (When he joined the Volunteers, Clarke and MacDermott told Wyse-Power that he was more useful to the movement as a lawyer than a Volunteer, and he went on to defend many Volunteers between 1913 and 1919, including the men in Tullamore).

18 See introduction, p. 27. Later in the day, when the authorities carried out a raid on the shop attached to Liberty Hall, recalled Rosie Hackett of the Irish Citizen Army, James Connolly and Helena Molony arrived immediately, armed and ready. On seeing the police with the papers that they intended to confiscate, Connolly said: 'Drop them, or I will drop you.' The police were forced to withdraw and return later with a warrant.

19 This most likely refers to Thomas MacPartlin, who in 1916 was chairman of the Irish Trades' Union Congress and Labour Party, as well as a Trustee of the Dublin United Trades' Council.

MARCH, 1916.

Thursday 23

Seizure of Spark honesty jail
+ printing machinery taken
to castle, military & police armed
I th appearance of Military
Soldiering is an interesting occupation
It is not more dangerous than
repairing hours, no worry by tailors or
"touching" friends, I believe I am
developing the military instinct

Friday 24

3rd in Lent. Sunday 26

Meeting of Carpenters
proposed strike Resolution
Composed by Mc Parten, it
coincided with my views
only 2 dissentients. I believe I
am qualifying to become a
"Labor advocate" & saying opinion

Monday 27

Blythe, Mellows & Monahan to be expelled from Ireland.[20]

'contact with enemy' at several points. Our guards on the alert. Vol[trs] taking up positions 'within the law'.

Wednesday 29

Meeting of Carpenters.

Abrupt negotiations

How employers can play at objectivity [?]: Demand reduced

Another chat arranged, probable same result, patience is indeed a virtue, but only when exercised by free men. (I mean in mind)

Thursday 30

Meeting Mansion House re deportation of Blythe, Mellows and Monahan[21]

20 *The Irish Times* reported on Tuesday 28 March that Alfred Monaghan, along with 'Messrs. Ernest Blythe and Liam Mellowes [*sic*], organisers of the Irish Volunteers, have ... been notified that they must choose for residence some place in the Midlands of England, within six days'. Failure to do so would mean 'they will be forcibly deported from Ireland'. Blythe and Mellows were at that time being held in the Arbour Hill barracks.

21 Following the serving of the deportation orders, there was an upsurge in anti-government feeling, as many were enraged that an Irishman could be told he had to live outside Ireland. A meeting was arranged in Dublin's Mansion House, and President of the Volunteers Eoin MacNeill was the principal speaker. *The Irish Times* reported on 31 March that 'the speeches were of a strong character'. Volunteer John J. Styles recalled that 'some of the speakers called on the Volunteers to attack Arbour Hill and rescue [Blythe and Mellows]' (BMH WS 175, p. 10). Tensions were high that evening: a crowd of about 2,000 gathered outside after the meeting and blocked trams in Dawson Street. A pipers' band then led the crowd towards College Green, and as they passed an army recruiting office on

Thursday 30

Tension between Vol^trs and gov very __

Vols ready for immediate action

History in the making, staged [?] by guns & swords. And an assorted quantity at that.

Grafton Street some shots were fired. According to *The Times* on 1 April, 'A good many soldiers and officers in uniform were met and "boohs" were directed at them.' Outside Trinity College, the *Times* reported, 'some more revolver shots were discharged, and one of these, it is said, pierced a pocket in the overcoat of Inspector Barrett, D.M.P.', only being stopped by his notebook. The police then charged and the crowd dispersed. The *Times* letters pages also carried a letter from an Irish Fusilier who, home recovering from wounds received at Suvla Bay, was in a cab which was held up by the crowd coming from the Mansion House. 'Filthy epithets were hurled at me by these men, and at least one man spat at me,' he wrote, adding that, having seen his fellow countrymen die like men abroad, 'I feel that it is an outrage to the memory of my gallant comrades that such men as those who paraded Dublin last night should be allowed to be at liberty in Ireland.' Feelings were still running high on 9 April when another parade was held to protest the deportation orders – the *Times* reported on 15 April that 'When the procession was passing through St Stephen's Green a tram driver attempted to take his vehicle through between two companies ... A cyclist in Volunteer uniform placed his machine in front of the tram, placed his hand upon his revolver, and dared the driver to proceed. The tram man at once stopped until the whole procession had passed.' These events proved very useful to the Volunteers and Citizen Army in terms of gaining new recruits.

Friday 31

Meeting of Carpenters

Strike declared.[22] More fuel to the furnace of political disquiet. Where will it end? The devil knows!

APRIL

Saturday 1

'All fools day.' Who could be wise in Ireland today? 'Backsight' would appear a greater asset than 'foresight'.

The weather is improving, the day is fine & bracing, a fine day for a holiday.

No money for 'Digs' (in advance).

22 This decision carried an unusual risk for sixty-three of the carpenters, since they were 'engaged in the making of munitions of war' – specifically the construction of cases for the transport of artillery shells required for the war effort. With regular difficulties in meeting requirements and following a politically embarrassing crisis in 1915, when a shortage of artillery shells halted some British advances, the Munitions of War Act 1915 was introduced in August, which brought private companies under the control of the Ministry of Munitions. One effect was the suspension of trade union rights in those companies; it also became an offence for an employee to leave his job without his employer's permission and striking was illegal. These carpenters were taking a bigger gamble than their colleagues, as they risked prosecution for their actions. Their cases were eventually brought before the Dublin Munitions Tribunal on 18 April. The identity of one of the striking carpenters is known: John Dunphy, who was fatally shot on 28 April during the Rising. According to *The Irish Times*, 20 May 1916, 'He was a carpenter on strike, and was shot through the heart by a bullet discharged from a rifle in Messrs. Jacob's factory, which was then in possession of the rebels.'

MARCH—APRIL, 1916.

Friday 31

meeting of carpenters strike declared. more fuel to the furnace of political disquiet whose will in end? The devil knows!

Saturday April 1

"all fools day." Who could be wise in Ireland. Today? "Backsight" would appear a greater asset than "foresight" The weather is improving the day is fine ... a fine day for a holiday. no money for "Digs" ...

Sunday 02

Vol Parade.[23]

23 As there is no record of any major Volunteer parade on this date, it's likely that de Brún's note refers to a meeting of just his company or battalion, possibly in the Fr Mathew Park, Fairview.

Monday 3

Elected to Strike Committee

Debarred from sitting owing to arrears. Not sorry. Rule might have been suspended in my case

I believe I could have helped

some 'rivals' there I believe.

Afraid of me. Workers love liberty but a rule enslaves them.

Tuesday 4

Position.   No business doing

No money

No prospect of either

Strike in full sway

Must see it through.

Volunteers 'practically' standing to attention. Must not be absent.[24]

24 De Brún appears to be feeling the strain of his involvement with both the carpenters' strike and the rising tension associated with the Volunteer movement – it seems to have been clear that action was imminent, with the Volunteers apparently on constant standby. Nevertheless, by the end of the entry, de Brún seems to have come to terms with the situation.

It is good. I have no responsibility but that of meeting my creditors.

I owe them consideration & a lot more.

Thursday 6

Misfortunes never come singly. The adage proved.

Ineligibility for strike com. [committee] followed by decree of exclusion by O'Neill

Trades unionism & personalities allied in officials Liberty & tyranny cannot agree. <u>Some</u> Society officials love not me. What's the reason? It won't serve the strike movement

____ should be postponed at any rate.

Friday 7

Volunteer Recruiting Meeting[25]

O'Rathaile & McDonagh spoke[26]

The first rather foolishly [?] the second " [rather] vainly.

Will they stand by their defiance of government, if necessary? Perhaps![27]

---

25 Coming soon after the anti-deportation demonstration on 30 March, this meeting would probably have seen a consequent rise in recruits. Indeed, after the march held on 9 April, *The Irish Times* reported the next day that 'About 1,300 men participated in the march, and of these a proportion were recruits, who were said to have joined during the week, and who appeared on parade without equipment.'

26 Michael Joseph O'Rahilly (O'Rathaille) and Thomas MacDonagh were senior members of the Irish Volunteers.

27 Any doubt de Brún may have had about their convictions was soon removed: O'Rahilly died in a lane off Moore Street, having led a charge from the GPO, and MacDonagh, de Brún's senior officer in the Jacob's factory garrison, was executed on 3 May 1916.

APRIL, 1916.

Tuesday 4

Position . No business during
no money
no prospect of ath
Stable in full swing
must see it through.
Volunteers "practically" standing to
attention. must not be absent.
It is good. I have no responsibility but
that of meeting my creditors.

Wednesday 5

I owe them consideration & a
lotmore,

APRIL, 1916.

Thursday 6

misfortunes never come singly
the adage proved.
ineligibility for strike com. followed
by decree of exclusion by ONeill
Trades Lamourum & personalities
allied in officials liberty & tyranny
cannot opra. some society officials
are not me. what's the reason?
it wont serve the genefle movement
exclusion should be postponed
at any rate.

Friday 7

Volunteer Recruiting meeting
O Rariche & McDonagh spoke
the first rather foolishly
the second + vaudly
will they stand by their defiance
of government, if necessary. Perhaps!

Thursday 13

Members Tribunal.
63 carpenters charged
Case adjourned pending
decision given re return
to work

Saturday 08

17/- digs arrears

Tuesday 11

B. Coy. Coldness. The limit reached. Left early. Consider resignation.[28]

Thursday 13

Members Tribunal.

63 carpenters charged[29]

Case adjourned pending decision given re return to work

---

28 Unfortunately de Brún doesn't elaborate on this situation, but he is clearly considering resigning as adjutant of 'B' Company, 2nd Battalion.
29 See note 22.

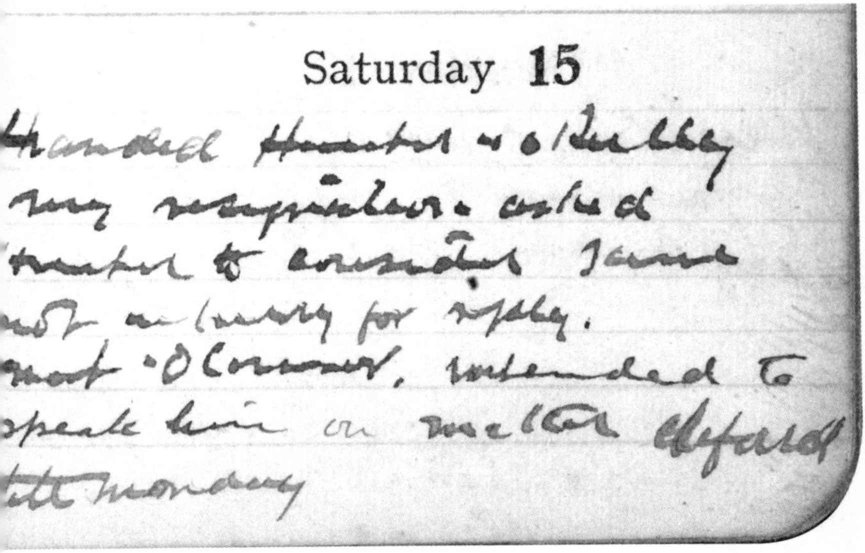

Saturday 15

[handwritten diary entry]

Saturday 15

Handed Hunter & O'Reilly my resignation & asked Hunter to consider same not as ___ for safety [?].

Met O'Connor, intended to speak him [sic] on matter deferred till Monday.

Sunday 16

J. Kenny borrowed 10/-

Owe him another 20/-

Landlady 1-2-0

If not hanged or drowned I will be strangled with debt.

A.W. —

APRIL, 1916.

Palm Sunday. **Sunday 16**

J. Kenny borrowed 10/-
over lnia another 20/-.

Landlady 1-8-0.
If not hanged or drowned I
will be strangled with debt.
A.W. ——

Monday 17

Mumtins trial of
Carpenters. Left it to
judgment in tomorrow

APRIL, 1916.

Tuesday 18 ○ ·

Judgement of internal
office find on left members
met obtained. gave him
copy of resignation of adjutancy

Wednesday 19

Corporation meeting. Kelly
speech + documents re preparations
against Volunteers. Our fellows setting
with "news"

Cabinet Crisis. English news
Everybody + Everybody is nervous
present time. all invalids

Monday 17

Munitions trial of carpenters. For 2 Hrs

Judgement in tomorrow

Tuesday 18

Judgement of Tribunal

2/6 fine on 43 members.[30]

Met O'Connor. Gave him copy of resignation of adjutancy

Wednesday 19

Corporation meeting. Kellys speech & documents re preparations against Volunteers.[31] Our fellows seething with '<u>nerves</u>'.

Cabinet crisis.[32] English nerves

---

30 The carpenters claimed that the shell cases they were making were not munitions and that they weren't munitions workers under the act. Nevertheless the Tribunal ruled that 'shell cases were as important a factor in the conclusion of this war as the shells they contained' and that forty-three of the men qualified as being engaged in munitions work. However, because of the manner in which the employers had handled the dispute, the carpenters were only fined two shillings and sixpence each, despite the fact that the Tribunal had the power to fine them up to five pounds per day – a figure that could have been catastrophic to a tradesman in 1916. Within a month, *The Irish Times* was able to report that an arbitrator had been appointed and the dispute settled to both parties' satisfaction.

31 Alderman Tom Kelly – see p. 28.

32 The cabinet crisis of April 1916 centred on the issue of recruiting and whether to make it generally compulsory or not, with differences of opinion amongst members of government causing grave concerns, at least in the press. On 19 April *The Irish Times* reported that a 'vital statement of fact and policy' is awaited, and that the government could fall as a result of the crisis, but added, 'We are very little concerned for the fate of the Coalition Government as compared with the issue of the war. We could find another Government, but the alternative to victory in this war is defeat and the end of Empire.' In fact nowadays the Easter

Everything & everybody is nervous

Present time all inwards

Thursday 20

Strike still on.

Cabinet crisis settled secret session of parliament, something wrong with the Empire.[33] '<u>Nerves</u>' perhaps!

Sunday 23 Easter Sunday

Mobilisation of Volunteers called off by Eoin MacNeill.[34]

Excitement intense. The crisis is near

Rising is often cited as the first step towards the end of Empire.

33 *The Irish Times* reported on 21 April that the cabinet crisis had ended, and the recruiting policy had been decided. The cabinet had agreed a set of proposals on recruiting which were to be 'submitted to a secret session in each House of Parliament', where facts and figures would be presented, 'of which publication must obviously be undesirable'.

34 Eoin MacNeill, founder member and chief of staff of the Irish Volunteers, having discovered that he had been deceived by members of the Irish Republican Brotherhood within his organisation, issued a general order to the Volunteers calling off manoeuvres on Easter Sunday, the original date set for the Rising to begin. It's clear from de Brún's note that expectations, and tensions, were high – his remark on the crisis being near was correct, and the rebellion went ahead the next day, albeit with a much-reduced turnout of Volunteers.

APRIL, 1916.

Easter Monday. Monday **24**

Going to Scalp with mother.
mobilisation unlikely. perhaps.
Return to city possible to meet
Eta Hussey etc. Emergency mobilisation & hurried movements
Barracks. New Street. Jacobs
occupied

"We are in action boys"

Tuesday **25**

Commandant Hunter says
we must fight & die to secure
for a free Irish Republic.
Excitement. fear. nervousness
amongst us at unexpected develop-
But action was inevitable.
Barricades in Blackpitts

APRIL, 1916.

Wednesday 26

intercept military. populace
dont understand execration
'Jews. prize fight between themselves
personal. ... are these the
people we are trying to free?
are they worth fighting for?
the dregs of the population.
they dont understand.
patience! they are the product
of misrule. If fighting for them
improves their condition
that alone consoles

Thursday 27

money has changed them
tomorrow they will cheer us.
Thank Heaven, ordered to
'fall back' to 'Jacobs', inside,
relief. darkness & nervousness
Jacobs is a vast place
a big place for a small number

Monday 24 Easter Monday

Going to Scalp with Mattie[35]

Mobilisation unlikely, perhaps.

Return to buy pamphlet. Meet Vols hurrying. Emergency mobilisation Excited & hurried movements

Barmacks, New Street, Jacobs occupied.[36]

'We are in action, boys' Commandant Hunter says.

We know fight & die is necessary [sic] for a free Irish Republic.

Excitement, fear, nervousness amongst us at unexpected development. But action was inevitable.

Barricades in Blackpitts[37]

Intercept military.[38] Populace don't understand, execration & jeers. Free fights between themselves.[39]

35 Mattie (Martha) Maguire – see p. 33.
36 'Barmack (limited), hop food specialists', 12 Fumbally's Lane – *Thom's Official Directory, 1917*. In statements to the Bureau of Military History, other Volunteers refer to it as Barmac's, and as a distillery or brewery.
37 Blackpitts is the name of a road parallel to Clanbrassil Street in Dublin.
38 Outposts were established around Jacob's with the intention of intercepting any troops that may have been sent from Portobello (now Cathal Brugha) Barracks.
39 Volunteer Michael Walker recalled that 'The inhabitants of Blackpitts were very hostile, singing and dancing to English songs of a quasi-patriotic type – pelted stones at us and generally showed great opposition which eventually culminated in an attack on a Volunteer by a man who formed one of the crowd with the object of disarming the Volunteer. This man was shot and bayonetted, I believe, fatally' (BMH WS 139, p. 4). Volunteer Vincent Byrne was possibly describing the same incident when he wrote that 'a lot of soldiers' wives and, I expect, imperialistic people – men and women – came around us. They jeered and shouted at us. One man in the crowd was very aggressive. He tried to take the rifle off one of our party. Lieutenant Billy Byrne told him to keep off or he would be sorry. The man, however, made a grab at the rifle. I heard

Imperial ____. Are these the people we are trying to free? Are they worth fighting for? The dregs of the population. They don't understand. Patience! They are the product of misrule. If fighting for them improves their condition that alone consoles. Maintenance money has changed them.[40]

Tomorrow they will cheer us.

Thank Heaven, ordered to 'fall back to Jacobs', inside, relief, darkness & nervousness.

Jacobs is a vast place

A big place for a small number of men to hold. Sleep in snatches.

Tuesday 25

Location. Preparation. Barricading. Strengthening our position. Volunteers brave & hopeful. Manly fellows.

P. Callan nervous.[41] Can't sleep & bad digestion. He was calm yesterday. Reaction I suppose today. I review my life. I believe I was fated to be here today. I could not have escaped it. It seems I was irresistibly drawn.

I was annoyed at mobilisation yesterday. It spoiled my anticipated day's outing. But 'man proposes' etc.[42]

a shot ring out and saw him falling at the wall' (BMH WS 423, p. 2). The women 'were like French revolution furies' according to Volunteer Thomas Pugh (BMH WS 397, p. 5).

40 This probably refers to the 'separation money' that wives of soldiers in the British Army received during the war while their husbands served.

41 The lists of rebel prisoners given in the *Sinn Féin Rebellion Handbook* show a P. Callan, carpenter, of 59 Millmount Avenue, Dublin. In the census of 1911, he gives his name as Pádraig Ua Cathaláin, so it's possible that Callan was both a union and a Gaelic League colleague of de Brún's.

42 The full proverb is: 'Man proposes, God disposes'.

APRIL, 1916.

of men which. They in made

Tuesday

~~Friday 28~~

location. Preparation.
Barracading everything
our position. Volunteers brave
+ hopeful. manly fellows
P. Callan nervous. kant slee
+ bad digestion, he was calm
yesterday reaction suppose
today. I review my life
I believe **Saturday 29** ated to
be here today. I could not
have escaped it It seems
I was irresistible drawn
I was annoyed at mobilisati
yesterday. It spoiled my anti
days outing. But "man propose
&c. Tuesday passes better sl
My night attack. men settl

APRIL—MAY, 1916.

down, now favourable, coming
in of spirits
we now thoroughly realise
our position and are
becoming reconciled to it
we believe we are going to
make a sacrifice, we offer
it to god & our country.

Low
Sunday. **Sunday 30**

Wednesday

I am well in advance of
my diary But now time
our time

Monday May 1

is not trouble is

our time is Irelands and
Irelands only Paddy
Callan is quite calm
today. Poor Pat. tells me
he did not expect to be
engaged in Revolutionc

85

Tuesday passes. Better sleep

No night attack. Men settling down, news favourable. Coming in often – keeps up our spirits.[43]

We now thoroughly realise our position and are becoming reconciled to it. We believe we are going to make a sacrifice. We offer it to god & our country.

Wednesday 26

I am well in advance of my diary.[44] But now time our time [sic] does not trouble us. Our time is Ireland's and Ireland's only. Paddy Callan is quite calm today. Poor Pat. Like me he did not expect to be engaged in Revolution at least so suddenly. We expected the offensive would be forced on us. Eoin MacNeill we hear is fighting as a private. Hobson and MacNeill did not favour revolt it appears.[45] Jas Connolly & Citizen Army doing splendid work.[46] MacDonagh, Hunter, McKee, All our

---

43 Several of the statements given to the BMH by members of the Jacob's garrison recall that dispatches arrived often. Volunteer Seamus Pounch stated that they 'received couriers hour by hour with details of the fighting which was now in full fury' (BMH WS 267, p. 11). However, not all of the men felt as well informed – Volunteer Pádraig Ó Ceallaigh recalled that 'Despatch riders had kept the Volunteer leaders in touch with the position in other parts of the city but we of the rank and file had only a dim idea as to what was happening elsewhere in Dublin and none at all of the position outside it' (BMH WS 376, p. 4). Nevertheless, at the time, de Brún was happy with the regular reports he was hearing.

44 This refers to the fact that this entry starts under the printed date of Sunday 30 May.

45 Despite being general secretary of the Irish Volunteers in 1916 and a member of the Supreme Council of the Irish Republican Brotherhood, Bulmer Hobson opposed the Rising and tried to prevent it.

46 James Connolly was commander of the Irish Citizen Army, but having been appointed Commandant-General of the combined rebel forces in Dublin, he was based in the GPO during the Rising.

fellows working wonderfully.[47] We are becoming 'soldiers' now. The Volunteer 'feeling' is past, we are now campaigners & we will make good ones. Some of our fellows quite young but magnificent courage. We are beginning to know each other ____ talk, fun & good spirits. **Tea** 'Hurry up up' [sic] Provisioning here is perfect tons of flour, sugar, & biscuits and those girls working so hard. Only in great moments like these does one get a true glimpse of Womanhood, patient, self-sacrificing & cheerfully brave.

I have been to confession.[48] First time for years. I feel better for it. I do believe that the Catholic Religion and Irish nationality are better in meaning than synonymous they are so interwoven. The spirit of Christ & Irish Nationality. The spirit of progress & sacrifice.

After tea. Inspection of position. Withdrawal to ____ do. Attack expected.[49] Men of our section nervous. Officers also apprehensive. This is the culminating point of our first experience. Over tonight & we will face anything.

I A.M. new barricades finished jaded tired. Sleep in equipment. No soft bed now.

---

47 Volunteer officer Dick McKee.
48 See p. 36.
49 With rumours circulating, and the sights and sounds of machine guns, artillery and infernos apparently getting closer as the week went on, the tension was high, and de Brún constantly refers to attacks that were expected, but never came. Volunteer Pádraig Ó Ceallaigh wrote that when the garrison surrendered, some were disappointed, but 'For some others there was, I think, a feeling of relief that the strain of the week was over; the strain on us was probably more intense because of our comparative inactivity. There was also the uncertainty.'

MAY, 1916.

at least so suddenly.
We expected the offensive
would be forced on us.

Tuesday 2 ●

Eoin MacNeill we hear is
fighting as a private. Hobson
& MacNeill did not favour Rev
it appears. Jas Connolly & City
Armies doing splendid work
McGee Donough Heuston, McD
All our fellows working wonder
fully. We are beginning "Soldi
now. The o . . . .

Wednesday 3

. . . . we are now campaign
& we will make good ones
some of our fellows quite young
but magnificent courage
We are beginning to know each
other . . . . talk fun
& good spirits. _Tea_ . . .
up

MAY, 1916.

up" Provisioning here is perfect
tons of Flour Sugar & Biscuits
and those girls working so

Thursday 4

hard. Only in great moments like
those does one get a true glimpse
of Womanhood, patient selfsacrificing
cheerfully brave,
I have been to confession.
first time for years. I feel better
or if I do beleive that the
Catholic Religion and a

Friday 5

Irish Nationality are better
in meaning than synonymous
they are so interwoven the
spirit of Christ & Irish Nationality
the spirit of progress & sacrifice
After tea. Inspection of
position withdrawal to

MAY, 1916

Saturday 6

to stoops do. Attack expected, men of our .... nervous officers also apprehensive. This is the culmination of our first experience. Over tonight & we will face anything.

1 A.M. new barricade finished. Jaded tired. Sleep in equipment. Soaked now.

Thursday

No attack a few hours improve. Real good wash & shave. A general inspection. Picking by myself the will to throw off.

2nd after Easter. **Sunday 7**

1st watch until 1 P.M.
Heavy firing on my front. Uncertain of old Building suspense, tension, Darkness & silence save for the

MAY, 1916.

Monday 8

rattle of rifles & Mr Christians
machine guns seen to be distinctly
clear. Plug Plug Plug — — — —
myriad soft sullen sounds
breaks perfunctory volleys
quiet to be recalled though
isode building.
guard ennobled. not fearsome
but highly strung. cool always
expecting attack. which does
not come

~~Tuesday 9~~

Friday
Com. Hunter always optimistic
officely cheery men overjoyed
sent to base for rest. Inside
arrangements very perfect
good supplies perfectly regular
and cross section recently.

Thursday 27

No attack. A few hours improved rest good wash & shave. A general inspection of factory by myself. It is well to know our whereabouts.

1st watch. Untill [sic] 1 P.M.

Heavy firing on my post, not certain if in Building. Suspense, tension. Darkness & silence save for the rattle of rifles & machine guns. Machine guns seem to be distinctive.[50]

Plug. Plug. Plug ....

Myriad soft sultry sounds of bullets perforating walls.

Expect to be riddled though inside building.

Guard ended, not fearsome but highly strung, can't sleep expecting attack, which does not come.

Friday 28

Com. Hunter always optimistic. Officers cheery men resigned. Sent to base for rest. Inside arrangements very perfect.[51] Food supplies perfectly regular. Red Cross section ready.

Girls singing national songs dressed in green.

Men dress in all sorts of costumes, dungarees look more like mechanics at work than soldiers. Plenty of new clothes, boots + Tobacco.[52]

---

50 John J. (Seán) Murphy recalled, 'A series of windows overlooked the Adelaide Hospital and were in view of the Tower in the Castle from where we were under fire … by machine guns' (BMH WS 204, p. 7).

51 The base de Brún refers to was probably the area mentioned by Volunteer Thomas Pugh 'on the top floor of Jacobs, where they had a rest-room and library, with a glass roof and glass windows' (BMH WS 397, p. 5).

52 Help from outside the factory came in various forms. Two sisters, Mary

If it was not for occassional [*sic*] sniping the Factory would remind one of a huge entertainment, everybody merry & cheerful.[53]

In the Civilian mind, it is a most intensely realistic change in which every element and [?] phase of life is apparent as the mind dwells on the actual situation the spirit of comradeship dominating all.[54]

and Anne Reynolds, who had a clothing business nearby, supplied many of the men with clothes during Easter Week (see p. 150, n. 11). In other instances, the rebels left the factory to get supplies. Volunteer Seamus Pounch recalled that he 'was detailed to lead a second patrol to obtain supplies of potatoes, bread, etc. I was handed a warrant signed by Thomas McDonagh [*sic*], headed – I, as an officer of the Irish Republican Army, is duly authorised, etc. ... I commandeered lard from Cavey's, Wexford St., and potatoes from Quinlisk's Stores, Cuffe St., and several trays of loaf bread. ... I conscripted civilian help [to carry these] and marched the convoy to Jacob's ... I got permission to reward the conscripts with two loaves apiece for their services' (BMH WS 267, p. 12). According to Séamas Ó Maitiú, in his history of Jacob's (p. 43), the rebels obtained plenty of provisions from the surrounding area, and 'they also had a quantity of boots and the contents of McEvoy's stores on Redmond's Hill, and Larkin's tobacco and chandlery stores, Wexford Street.' Towards the end of the week, it seems the garrison were preparing to provide their own food. Thomas J. Meldon remembered that 'the ovens were being got ready for baking when the order to surrender came' (BMH WS 134, p. 14). In fact some may have already been experimenting, because, according to Ó Maitiú (p. 48): 'In 1961, at an exhibition night held by the Old Dublin Society, two burnt biscuits were displayed. It was said that they were made in Jacob's factory by some young volunteers who could not resist making them during Easter Week despite being told not to touch machinery. They were burnt to a cinder, but the company name was still legible.'

53 Things were evidently quiet within the factory – so much so that according to Pounch, 'During a lull in the fighting in Jacob's we held a miniature ceilidh – Volunteers and Fianna, Cumann na mBan, Clan na Gael Girl Scouts ... and [it] was a real welcome break in the serious business we had on hands' (BMH WS 267, pp. 12–13).

54 It's unclear what de Brún is referring to here, and this sentence may simply illustrate the mental strain the men of the garrison were under.

girls singing national Song
reopened in green
men dressed in all sorts
of costumes, ... look

MAY, 1916.

Wednesday 10

more like mechanics at work
than soldiers, Plenty of New
clothes boots & Tobacco.
If it was not for occasional
singing The Factory would
remind one of a huge institute
everybody merry & cheerful

Thursday 11

In the Cinema mind it is
most intensely realistic cha
in which every element
phase of life is apparent
the mind dwells on the
actual situation the spirit
comradeship dominating all
approaching 12 o'clock

resting at base in luxurious improvised
settees. If reports of hospital.
the boys discussing the the chances
the rumours & the probabilities
of the red **Friday 12** Politics municip[al]
local National & International.
People personalities & figures.
May the Republic endure,
Ireland will endure.
Freedom has been asserted,
& Ireland has advanced to
a higher & I believe a holier
phase of her Destiny.

MAY, 1916.

Friday 12

Saturday 13

Afternoon passes quietly
Refreshed after rest
Reading, Smoking & playing
cards to music of gramophone
& Piano. Great temptation
to smoke but then I would break
my resolution & the terms of which

now are on the *tops* of
traps & in the *trenches* of
rifles

MAY, 1916.

3rd after Easter. ~~Sunday 14~~

Saturday. Called early
& selected *8pm* "Diverting
party." De Valera *at* *well*
Now hard pressed 14 *cyc*
all ready, we *proceed* to
places named. York St *St*
south, *carrion* *st* *town*
various *Sgt* *book* *Butler*
hospitals.

Monday 15

soldiers at *each* Sgt *Osin*
spread fire *remount*
return our *fellows* *of* *an*
col, back *same direction*
gauntlet *of shots,* via *York*
snipes at *top* *foster St.*

MAY, 1916.

Tuesday 16

Grady shot here, helped
along down to the post
col. if suspicious but a by
suspicious & went to factory
I did not think I would
return.

Easy day. read portion
"Julius Cæsar" Shakespeare
following the advice of himself
ones, Cassius' & Brutus'
interesting study, this is
he 1st Shakespeare copy

Wednesday 17 ○

saw & it is my favourite
the friendship honesty Reconciliation
B & C. is a beautiful expression
manly love, an ideal conception
the idea of the Brotherhood of men
and free from cant or cheap
political platitude.

Approaching 12 o'clock.

Resting at base on luxurious improvised settees. It suggests an hospital

The boys discussing the the [sic] chances the rumours & the probabilities of the revolution. Politics municipal local. National & International. People personalities & figures.

May the Republic endure, Ireland will endure.

Freedom has been asserted.

Ireland has advanced to a higher & I believe a holier phase of her Destiny.[55]

Afternoon passes quietly.

Refreshed after rest.

Reading. Smoking[56] & playing cards to music of gramophone & piano.[57] Great temptation to smoke but then I would break my resolution the terms of which now are on the __ of the gods & in the breeches of our rifles.

Saturday 29

Called early & selected to form 'Diverting party'. De Valera

---

55 De Brún's pencil changes here, from black to almost purple.
56 Ó Maitiú's history of Jacob's quotes an account of the Rising found in Jacob's archives which tells that caretaker Thomas Orr asked rebel Commandant MacDonagh to prevent smoking in the factory as far as possible. According to the account, orders were immediately issued for smoking to cease – however, it's clear that at least in the base (or rest room) that de Brún refers to, smoking continued.
57 Volunteer Lieutenant John MacDonagh (brother of Comdt Thomas MacDonagh) recalled later: 'Some of the Volunteers discovered an old-fashioned gramophone, in a corner downstairs in Jacob's, that played *God save the King* and one day when Tom and MacBride were making their tour of inspection it was put on to take a rise out of them' (BMH WS 219, p. 2).

at Westland Row hard pressed. 14 cyclists are ready.[58] we proceed to the places named, York St, St Gn[59] south, Leeson St towards Merrion Sq past Red Cross hospitals.[60]

Soldiers at end of Sqr. Dismount opened fire remount return. Our fellows awful cool, back same direction, gauntlet of shots. Via York St.

Snipers at top Grafton St.

O'Grady shot here, helped along down York St past Col. of Surgeons held by our fellows & back to factory.

I did not think I would return.[61]

Easy day. read portion of 'Julius Caesar' Shakespeare following the advice of Irish Times.[62] 'Cassius & Brutus' interesting study. This is the 1st Shakespearean play I saw & it is my favourite.

The Friendship, Quarrel & Reconciliation

B & C is a beautiful expression of manly love, an ideal conception of the idea of the Brotherhood of man and free from cant or cheap political platitude.

---

58 See *A Sortie from Jacob's*, p. 134.
59 St Stephen's Green.
60 In 1916 there was a War Hospital Supply Depot in 40 Merrion Square.
61 De Brún appears to have initially written 'should' here, but crossed out the 'sh' and replaced it with 'w'.
62 This casual reference is particularly interesting. When martial law was declared on Thursday 27, *The Irish Times* editorial asked: 'What is the fire-side citizen to do with those hours?' Among other suggestions, it recommended: 'Best of all, perhaps, he can acquire, or re-acquire, the art of reading … How many citizens of Dublin have any real knowledge of the works of Shakespeare? Could any better occasion for reading them be afforded than [this] enforced domesticity …?' This, then, is the 'advice of Irish Times' that de Brún is referring to just two days after it was printed, showing that within the Jacob's garrison, there was access to a daily newspaper, if not on the day of publication, then very soon after.

ORIGINAL

BUREAU OF MILITARY HISTORY 1913-21
BURO STAIRE MILEATA 1913-21
NO. W.S. 312

ROINN COSANTA.

BUREAU OF MILITARY HISTORY, 1913-21.

STATEMENT BY WITNESS

DOCUMENT NO. W.S. 312

Witness

Seosamh de Brun,
70 Irishtown Road,
Sandymount,
Dublin.
Identity

Member of 'B' Company, 2nd Battalion,
Dublin Brigade Irish Volunteers 1916.

Subject

The Easter Week Rising 1916 -
Jacob's Factory.

Conditions, if any, stipulated by Witness

Nil

File No. S.1283

Form B.S.M. 2.

The cover of Seosamh de Brún's statement to the Bureau of Military History. Reproduced courtesy of the Military Archives.

TRANSCRIPT OF SEOSAMH DE BRÚN'S STATEMENT TO THE BUREAU OF MILITARY HISTORY, 22 OCTOBER 1949

Written more than thirty-three years after the Rising, de Brún's statement to the Bureau of Military History provides a fascinating counterpoint to his diary, written in the moment. The diary is clearly written for an audience of one, with personal notes and passionate comments, all written quickly and without much in the way of obvious self-editing. The statement to the Bureau is just the opposite. Differences in the two accounts are to be expected, given the passage of years, but the 1949 statement was very definitely written for a larger audience and has all the appearances of a document crafted with an eye to the writer's place, or at least involvement, in history.

De Brún is big on the glory associated with the rebellion and striking a blow for Irish freedom, but somewhat vaguer when it comes to his own, and indeed the Jacob's garrison's, contribution to the rebellion. He writes that 'it is evident that though all the other units of command were incessantly fighting, defending and consolidating their positions ... Jacob's factory and its environs was the scene of military activities during the Week, the importance of which, I believe, has not yet been realized in connection with the whole story of the Rising.' And although he describes how the Rising ended for the Jacob's garrison, he unfortunately didn't avail of the opportunity to describe how his own Rising ended, merely stating: 'Numbers of the men were given the option to escape from the building and availed of it.'

Nevertheless, because both the diary and the later witness statement are now available, we not only have the unique opportunity to get a glimpse of the rebellion as it was happening, but we also have the chance to compare a 1916 Volunteer's on-the-spot notes, written under fire, with his considered recollections of some decades later. As mentioned, there are some differences, but it's fascinating to see the similarities across the years – the feelings, the emotions and the enthusiasm remain evident, despite the passage of years. Here then, is de Brún's statement to the Bureau of Military History:[1]

ROINN COSANTA.
BUREAU OF MILITARY HISTORY, 1913–21.
STATEMENT BY WITNESS
DOCUMENT NO. W.S. 312

Witness

Seosamh de Brun,
70 Irishtown Road,
Sandymount,
Dublin.

1   Seosamh de Brún's statement was made on 22 October 1949, and is repro-
    duced here with permission. Original spellings and punctuation have been
    retained, even where these are inconsistent, e.g. Boland's/Bolands.

Identity
Member of 'B' Company, 2nd Battalion,
Dublin Brigade Irish Volunteers 1916.

Subject
The Easter Week Rising 1916 –
Jacob's Factory.

Conditions, if any, stipulated by Witness
Nil

File No. S.1283
Form B.S.M. 2.

STATEMENT BY SEOSAMH DE BRÚN
70 Irishtown Road, Sandymount, Dublin.

Easter Sunday morning, April 23rd., was fixed for a general mobilisation of the Dublin Brigade, Irish Volunteers. Intense and somewhat anxious interest was centred in the event, particularly after the reported sinking of the 'Aud' laden with munitions off the coast of Kerry and the sensational arrest of Sir Roger Casement on Good Friday. Many divined that a crucial period was developing, the call to duty was regarded as inexorable in view of those incidents. Consequently whatever arrangements I personally had or was inclined to make for spending the holidays in the usual manner, required to be of a tentative character. The countermanding of the general mobilisation order early

Sunday morning by Commandant Eoin MacNeill gave rise to speculation to which increasing rumours of various kinds lent added zest. Although the general parade was called off many of the Company opined that it was only postponed, and an instantaneous mobilisation might be ordered at any moment during the coming week; in fact it was even expected that evening, so perfect was the military system of the Volunteers that immediate mobilisation was only a matter of a couple of hours. With those ideas in mind I reported to 2nd Battalion Headquarters, Fairview Park, that afternoon where I saw Commandant Thomas Hunter and other members of B. Company, to which I was attached. Ammunition was being distributed, no mobilisation was likely that evening though, perhaps, not improbable.[2]

Easter Monday morning gave promise of an ideal holiday. Brilliant sunshine and warm dry weather invited one to the mountains or seaside. Turning over in my mind which I should choose, as I left the house,[3] I noticed at the corner of Seville Place a group of Volunteers in uniform.[4] Seems like a Company mobilisation I thought. Going over I asked was such the case, they replied they had

2   In his 1937 sworn evidence to the Advisory Committee, Military Service Pensions Act, 1934, de Brún stated that on Easter Sunday 'we were down in Fairview Park distributing ammunition' for 'practically all the afternoon'.

3   According to his diary, de Brún was going to the Scalp with Mattie Maguire, his future wife.

4   The corner of Seville Place and Amiens Street would have been visible from de Brún's front door at No. 72 Amiens Street.

orders to mobilise. I decided to go to Fairview Park and at Newcomen Bridge met Captain Weafer cycling towards the city.[5] Hailing him I enquired if the parade was general.[6] 'Yes', replied the Captain 'get over to Stephen's Green the 2nd Battalion mobilises there at 11 o'clock'. I will be late for this parade I thought, for it wanted only a couple of minutes to the hour. I went back 'hot foot' to the house in Amiens Street,[7] stripped myself hurriedly of holiday attire and got into service rig. I took the precaution of taking extra accoutrement,[8] for somehow I felt anything might happen though the actual Rising was far from my thoughts.[9] I jumped on a tram to the Pillar, another to Stephen's Green. I got there at 11.20. A large number of Volunteers had assembled, others were arriving, the mobilisation I perceived had only begun. The usual group of sightseers were watching us amongst whom I noticed Detective 'Johnny Barton' of the G. Division, an interested spectator. Johnny was a well known figure to Gaels. He was killed during the fighting that took place preceding the Treaty.[10] He was credited with having identified Sean

5 Captain Thomas Weafer was killed at the corner of O'Connell Street and Lower Abbey Street on Wednesday 26 April.

6 In his 1937 statement, de Brún remarks that 'the man who was sent to mobilise me met with an accident, and I met Captain Thomas Weafer'.

7 Newcomen Bridge is about 300 metres from No. 72 Amiens Street.

8 Among the extras that he took with him, de Brún included his diary, but it's impossible to say whether he did so out of habit or because he intended to document the Rising.

9 This is somewhat at odds with his diary, in which, several times, de Brún mentions the growing tension and feeling of anticipation, for example on Sunday: 'Excitement intense. The crisis is near.'

10 Barton was a notorious police detective and is mentioned many times in

MacDiarmuidha, McBride and others after the 'Cease Fire' in Easter Week.

There was a mixed assemblage of numerous Companies on Stephen's Green. I joined those of B. Company. About 12 o'clock, Commandants Hunter, McDonagh and other officers were moving briskly about; suddenly we got the order to 'fall in' and 'quick march'.[11] We 'Right turned' into Cuffe Street and in somewhat loose military order proceeded to Kevin Street. Alongside those I marched was Sam Ellis on a hackney car, his arms around a large heavy-looking box which I surmised was ammunition. When we came to Jacob's Factory, part of the troops commanded by Commandant Thomas McDonagh took possession of the building: the large section in which I was marched to cross Kevin Street past the Police Barracks to New Street, down Fumbally's Lane where we took possession of Barmacks buildings which we put immediately into a state of defence. Extra ammunition was distributed. On the top floor, where the windows commanded the approach to Blackpitts, we were paraded by Commandant Thomas Hunter who in a short characteristic address said 'Men! The Irish Republic has been proclaimed in Dublin to-day; we are in action; the Headquarters of the Irish Republican Army is at the General Post Office, which has been taken possession of by the Republican troops. We are fighting

various statements to the BMH. He was assassinated in November 1919, outside what is now Pearse Street garda station.

11 De Brún's statement consistently refers to 'McDonagh', whereas in the diary, he correctly writes 'MacDonagh'.

to establish the Irish Republic. I trust every man here will give loyal and obedient service and will acquit himself as a gallant soldier in the cause of Irish Independence'. We were standing to attention. We relaxed; a loud cheer rang through the building, some saluted, others raised their guns: one, a recruit evidently, called for spiritual ministration, thinking he was going to be sent at once before his Maker. An order was issued, windows were smashed, glass crashed, rifles were t[h]rust out in search of appropriate positions; the realisation we were in action was swiftly upon us. A squad was moved to the corner of Mill Street, another facing Blackpitts. A coachbuilder's yard at the corner was forced open and the lumber taken to form barricades. The people of the neighbourhood gathered with lively curiosity. They seemed at a loss to know whether we were in action or merely on manoeuvres: as the day wore on they too began to realise the seriousness of their position especially when a tall Volunteer not quite seasoned to arms during a false alarm that the British were approaching let his Howth gun fall to the ground, a charge was released with a report that made his comrades as well as a number of the people jump with the shock. It was the first shot, though an accidental one, fired by our lot. One chap declared it nearly took the tip of his ear off. After this the people kept a respectful distance, though numbers considered at the time to be British soldiers' dependents [sic] or sympathisers were definitely hostile. Several times they essayed to tear down the barricades, our men displayed great good temper. They seemed to know those people did not understand,[12] at times patience became brittle and but for the knowledge that they were of the prolatariate [*sic*] reprisals might have followed.[13] It was the first real lesson in actual discipline we learned, it was justified, as before the week was out those very people were madly enthusiastic in the cause of the Irish Republic.

During the day we had tea made for us by two ladies who lived near by named O'Byrne, (I think).[14] Towards evening the rawness of our initiation to active service began to wear off though the strain of expectancy was still with us.[15] About 7 o'clock we got the order to retire from Barmacks, which it seems had only been occupied as an outpost, to intercept troops coming from Portobello Barracks.[16] Apparently it was regarded as of no further immediate strategic value. We retired with our prisoners, two police officers, through New Street, cross Kevin Street to Jacob's factory.

Jacob's factory

In the factory we found a strenuous atmosphere. Instead

---

12 This mirrors de Brún's diary notes, where he writes plaintively: 'Are these the people we are trying to free? Are they worth fighting for? The dregs of the population. They don't understand. Patience!'

13 In fact, as noted above, other Volunteers remembered that a man who tried to disarm a Volunteer was shot, possibly fatally. It's possible that de Brún didn't witness the incident, but it's also possible that he deliberately chose not to mention it.

14 Tea is referred to fondly in both the diary and witness statement.

15 The diary describes this as: 'We are becoming "soldiers" now. The Volunteer "feeling" is past.'

16 The diary says simply: 'Barricades in Blackpitts. Intercept military.'

of the spick and span citizen soldiery as they would
appear on parade, the garrison had the appearance of a
laborious day's toil. Barricades were raised on windows,
doorways and other points of defence, men were moving
about covered with flour from head to toe, many hatless,
some with coats off, actually engaged in the work of forti-
fication, others were already in position awaiting the
enemy. Officers moved briskly about issuing orders. With
their various arms and equipment the garrison presented
a strangely incongruous appearance. Some were dressed in
full uniform, the green showing pale beneath its mist of
flour in striking contrast with the civilian garb of others,
with cavalry bandolier, or canvas ammunition pouch, ration
bag or other serviceable equipment. The assorted types of
rifles, the devastating double-barrelled shot-gun, the crack
Winchester repeater, and latest pattern Lee Enfield British
service magazine rifle and bayonet, or the most powerful
of all, the Howth rifle fitted with long curved French
bayonet, together with small arms from point 32.c[alibre]
to German parabellum,[17] the whole ensemble suggested a
scene that could only be pictured by reading a description
– say Carlyle's, of the French Revolution,[18] yet not near so

17 All the rebel garrisons suffered from the same problem – a varied array
    of different calibre weapons, and not enough ammunition. Volunteer
    Seamus Pounch wrote of the Jacob's garrison: 'The weapons we had
    were mixed and represented every class of gun and revolver used by
    Volunteers; to this was added tin can bombs …' (BMH WS 297, p. 11).
    Some Volunteers in the various garrisons were armed with nothing more
    than pikes.
18 *The French Revolution: A History* by Thomas Carlyle, first published in
    1837, and famous for its vivid style of writing.

vivid in description as the actual appearance of revolution presented before our gaze. We were escorted to positions. The boiler house with its red tiled floor was our first post.

McDonagh's address

After some time we were called, together with other units on a general parade and addressed by Commandant McDonagh. In picturesque language, of which he was master, he gave an account of the Rising as it developed during the day, of the reinforcements marching to our aid from outlying districts, of allies landings on various parts of the coast, and of the reports that German submarines had formed a cordon around the country which effectually menaced any attempt on the part of the British to reinforce their Garrisons with the aid of the British fleet.[19] He also paid tribute to the magnificent qualities of soldierly discipline and energy displayed by the troops under his command, he made particular reference to the men who took possession and were fortifying Jacobs amongst whom he singled out Eamon (Mac 'e) Comerford[20] and Volunteer P. McDonnell[21] and promoted them Lieutenants for distinguished service. Major McBride who had joined

19 All unfounded rumours, unfortunately for the rebels.
20 Volunteer Seán Price mentions an 'M Comerford' of 'B' Company, 1st Battalion, as having fought in Jacob's, referring also to 'Mockie' Comerford (BMH WS 769). De Brún is giving his spelling of the nickname 'Mockie'. Another statement, by Volunteer Thomas Pugh (WS 397), mentions 'Monty Comerford', while William James Stapleton (WS 822) mentions 'Andy (Mocky) Comeford'. See also *Escape from Jacob's*, p. 153.
21 Patrick McDonnell.

in the operations of the day was formally promoted to the rank of Commandant, in which capacity he was of invaluable service during the occupation.

Commandant McBride also addressed us in inspiring language. The encouraging words of those two splendid personalities had a buoyant effect on the men, the seriousness of the situation was forgotten in the spirit of adventure. Cheers and cries of 'long live the Republic' rang throughout the building. It was a memorable scene in this dimly lit factory with its vast machinery shrouded with dust wraps, carefully placed by the workers ere they left off on the previous Saturday.[22] It was now about dusk and the shadows were beginning to glimmer. Seamus Ó h-Aodha was evidently guide or inspector of positions and he led our section to a billet for the night.[23] It was the engine room and boiler house at the base of the big chimney. The atmosphere was pleasantly warm and we threw ourselves on the tiled floor and tried to sleep for a while.[24] The next

22 According to Ó Maitiú's history of Jacob's, a small number of workers were present on the Bank Holiday Monday to carry out maintenance that could only be done when the machines were off. When the rebels broke in, the workers were placed under guard, and later allowed to leave. At least three employees stayed behind, however, including the caretaker, Thomas Orr (who lived next door to the factory on Peter Street), and the watchman on duty, Henry Fitzgerald (who lived somewhat further away on Ben Eadair Road, Stoneybatter).

23 This is probably James J. Hughes, the Gaelic Leaguer who organised the 1914 meeting in Wynn's Hotel – see p. 23.

24 Volunteer Thomas Pugh wrote that while in prison in Knutsford: 'Some of the fellows were a bit verminous from lying around the ovens in Jacobs and the authorities took our clothes and fumigated them' (BMH WS 397, p. 12).

picket was to report at the end of 4 Hrs. The inclination to sleep wore away after a while on the hard floor, most of us had visions of blankets and snug mattresses, and then there was something uncomfortably threatening about that big chimney shaft.[25] 'Suppose' said Pat Callan 'a shell struck it and the damn thing crashed'. It was most improbable at this stage it would occur, but the thought was disconcerting, the heat was telling on us. We were half dozing already. After a while of fitful sleep I was called to guard duty.

The next day (Tuesday) was spent erecting barricades with sacks of flour. The horses in the stables were removed to safety in case of fire. A squad was soon busy there smashing through walls making thorough communication to the outside of the building. Inflammable materials were removed as a precaution against incendiary shells. During the progress of this work we were begrimed with dust and sweat, coats off, rifles within easy reach, we worked as never we did before. Big Sergeant Pádraig Cathalain, for he held this rank during Easter Week, a carpenter by trade, with a sledge hammer in his brawny fists driving a steel bar through the brickwork, others punching with heavy levers, more cleaning away the debris, carrying bricks, a scene of determined laborious activity in which danger was forgotten.[26] Amidst

25 'Sleep in equipment. No soft bed now,' de Brún wrote in his diary.
26 In 1937 Pádraig Ua Cathaláin supplied a statement in support of de Brún's military service application. In it he stated that de Brún was 'adjutant of B. Co, 2nd Batt.' adding that 'I was sergeant of No. 1 Section same Co.' Pádraig Ua Cathaláin is mentioned several times in de Brún's diary as Paddy, or Pat, Callan.

the quip and crack of a joke, direct communication, without being exposed to rifle fire was made with the main building. Barbed wire entanglements were erected in the yard to trap the feet of the unwary invader. By Wednesday the entire factory was in a state of perfect defence against a hand to hand attack from any exposed point.[27]

Notwithstanding this it was clear a few well directed shells would have made Jacobs a death-trap for the Garrison. On the other hand suppose an attempt was made to take the place by assault, what carnage might have occurred around those machines on the ground floor. The fighting would be of a desperate nature.[28] A few of the squad toyed with the grindstones in the Machine shop, sharpened bayonets and penknives for the twofold purpose of shearing the enemy and rations. Speculations about the military value of the Factory were interrupted by orders to erect barricades at various interior passages. Our position faced the Adelaide Hospital and Bishop Street.

Incessant rifle fire was exchanged with snipers,[29]

27 The rebels also filled any available containers with water, in case of the supply being cut off.
28 In fact the factory was never attacked and the military were effectively able to bypass it as they closed their cordon around the city. The surrender came before a decision on whether to attack had to be taken, and with the entire surrounding area a mass of small houses, any attack, whether direct assault or artillery bombardment, would have been hugely costly in human life.
29 Sniping from the top of the factory was the main military action that the garrison engaged in. The factory's height gave the rebel snipers views over large swathes of the city. William James Stapleton recalled that 'During the week there was regular sniping from Portobello Barracks direction and continuous reply from the roof of the [factory] building' (BMH

together with gunfire from the College of Surgeons held by the Countess Markiewitz and Commandant Mallon, and attacks and defence of outposts.[30] This continued day and night, a slight lull in the dark hours before dawn, broken by occasional interchange by alert snipers, to increase in intensity at dawn when we were always 'standing too' against attack.[31]

The Factory was at this time in an admirable state of military organisation.[32] A rest base had been prepared where drafts from all the sections in turn were sent for a day's rest and recreation. The base was supplied with blankets, mattresses, pillows &c. brought in by the foraging parties. After nights lying on tiled or metal floors, the strenuous exertion erecting defences, exciting rushes to attention, the men reclined, smoked, read and chatted, some wrote diaries of events to date. This rest was a real relaxation, every man came away from it refreshed in mind and body.

WS 822, p. 6). Seamus Pounch wrote that 'The snipers were constantly attacking troops from every angle and causing a lot of confusion to the enemy before they were finally located. Portobello Bridge became a no-man's land for British sentries or troops' (BMH WS 267, p. 12). Michael Walker mentioned that 'Continuously during the week sniping went on from the buildings which we occupied with what results, of course, I cannot say' (BMH WS 139, p. 6).

30 Commandant Michael Mallin was the leader of the Stephen's Green garrison, with Countess Markievicz as his second-in-command.

31 As mentioned in the diary, the constant threat of attacks, particularly before dawn, put tremendous strain on the garrison.

32 With no actual attacks, and with ample supplies and materials to hand in the vast Jacob's factory, the garrison's situation was more akin to a barracks than an occupied stronghold prepared for assault.

A supply store and canteen under the supervision of Hannrai Ó hAnnracháin was plentifully provided with clothing, boots, tobacco and commodities that made for personal comfort displayed on long benches.[33] The store was much appreciated, underclothing, socks &c. were a boon to many, after three days of almost 24 hours continuous activity in complete original attire, through which flour and grime had penetrated to cake in sweaty shirts, without even removing our boots. The luxury of washing one's feet in a bucket, a new pair of socks, a pair of new boots and we felt we could march to the Wicklow hills and fight every inch of the way, if necessary. To add to those conveniences another and more homely service manifested itself by the active participation in the commissariat department of the Cumann na mBan amongst whom I recognised Maire Ni Siublaigh,[34] Mrs. O'Daly and others I now forget.[35] Our repetition diet of biscuits and sweets was soon replaced by

33 Henry O'Hanrahan, brother of Michael O'Hanrahan, both of whom appear alongside de Brún in the St Patrick's Day 1913 photograph on p. 22. Michael was nominal second-in-command to Thomas Mac-Donagh (replaced in practice by the late arrival of John MacBride) and was executed on 4 May. Henry was sentenced to life imprisonment.

34 Máire Nic Shiubhlaigh, one of the Cumann na mBan women with the Volunteers in Jacob's.

35 It's likely that de Brún is misremembering here. Mrs Nora O'Daly wrote an account of her experiences during the Rising for the 3 April 1926 edition of *An t-Óglách* magazine. She was indeed with the Cumann na mBan section which was attached to the 2nd Battalion (de Brún's battalion, which may be how he knew her). However, following the confusion created by the countermanding order and the postponement of the rebellion's start, O'Daly spent the week with the Stephen's Green/ College of Surgeons garrison.

more palatable rations of vegetables and meat.[36] How much of the personal comforts were provided for the Garrison by those courageous women can not be estimated, their appearance on the scene must have largely contributed to this side of the organisation of the Factory. A piano was strummed occasionally in an upper portion of the building in contrast with the rifle fire. The book-case in the library was broken open and pillaged. I can distinctly remember the interest evoked by quotations from 'Julius Caesar',[37] the battle of Pharsalia, etc.[38] Joe Thunder, Seamus Ó Maolfhainn,[39] Frank Kearney,[40] Mick Slator,[41] – Tom Pugh, Peadar Ó Cearnaigh to mention a few made a study circle during fatigue hours.[42] It reminded one of a school rather

36 As mentioned in the diary footnotes, foraging parties were occasionally sent out from the factory – Vincent Byrne recalled that at one point: 'We were running short of milk, and a forage party was sent out … The next thing I saw was Jimmy Slattery coming down the street with a milk-cart with two churns on it' (BMH 423 p. 4). According to Peadar Kearney, 'One thing which made ample amends for the attitude of the women on Monday was the generosity of people in the neighbourhood who, as long as it was possible, handed in supplies of milk and cigarettes – a veritable Godsend.' Quoted in de Burca, *The Soldier's Song*, p. 121.

37 Comments on *Julius Caesar* were the last notes that de Brún wrote in his diary before escaping from Jacob's.

38 The Battle of Pharsalia was fought in 48 BC. Julius Caesar, with about 30,000 men, faced Pompey the Great, who commanded more than 60,000. Despite the overwhelming odds, the battle was a resounding success for Caesar, so it's not hard to see why the tale would be of interest to a rebel audience in 1916.

39 Seamus Ó Maoilfhinn, who in 1937 supplied a statement in support of de Brún's military service application.

40 Frank Kearns.

41 Michael Slater.

42 Peadar Kearney, who wrote the lyrics for the Irish national anthem, *The Soldier's Song* (*Amhrán na bhFiann*).

than a war camp. Nor was humour lacking, every day a diminutive soldier of the Fianna Éireann both in stature and years – the youngest recruit I believe of the heroic boys who fought with us armed with double barrelled shot gun slung over his shoulder escorted two stalwart six foot odd policemen prisoners to the helpful task of peeling potatoes for the troops. This daily parade as it passed brought smiles to the faces of many if not to the prisoners.[43] 'Fancy' said some one, 'the ignominy to which two pillars of the most detested force in the British imperial administration in Ireland had been reduced. Had not the tables turned? the baton no longer held sway. Oh memories of 1913, the armed citizen has appeared, the National Will prevails.'[44]

By this time the entire Factory presented the appearance of a well organised military base, the periodical inspections of the positions by Commandants McDonagh, McBride and staff convinced us that thorough organisation and discipline were desired and obtained.[45] Everybody

43 This was probably Vincent Byrne, 14 or 15 at the time, who in his statement to the Bureau in 1950, wrote that he was 'put on guard over two policemen in the factory. It must have been a strange sight indeed to see the two men, six-foot high, looking down on the young lad of about four feet who was guarding them' (BMH 423 p. 3). Byrne was later to take part in the assassination of Johnny Barton, the police detective that de Brún noticed taking particular interest in the Volunteers assembling at Stephen's Green.

44 This is referring to the baton charges associated with the Dublin Lockout, the workers' strike of 1913.

45 De Brún seems almost overly concerned with emphasising the preparedness of the Jacob's garrison – perhaps this is in some way to offset the fact that it was never called on to prove its worth in actual fighting. Here he says 'the entire Factory presented the appearance of a well organised military base'. Elsewhere he mentions that 'the entire

had settled down to particular duties. Forage parties were active, communication with outside Forces was well maintained, Micheal Ó Caomhanaigh and Michael Ó hAodha were frequently seen on return from reconnoitring duties and gave information of the fighting in other parts of the city and country, of the defence of Davy's Public-house at Portobello bridge which held up any attempt by the British troops to leave Portobello barracks, of the death of Risteárd Ó Cearbhaill in Camden Street or Harcourt Street,[46] of the fierce fighting around King Street and the burning of Linenhall Military Barracks by Republican forces under the command of Commandant O'Daly, the occupation and defence of the Mendicity buildings, the terrific fighting in the Marrowbone Lane Distillery under Commandant Eamon Kent,[47] of the Battle of Ashbourne and the victory of the Republican troops: those stories and rumours of other developments were many such as the appearance of the loyalist veterans on the streets co-operating with the British, and the heavy losses inflicted by Commandant De Valera on the enemy advancing from Kingstown, were told us in language which aroused enthusiasm for our cause. Thus the days passed, sniping was causing us trouble, some of our crack shots were brought to the tower which dominated the area, Ned

factory was in a state of perfect defence.' And later: 'The Factory was at this time in an admirable state of military organisation.'

46 Dublin Councillor Richard O'Carroll was fatally wounded in Camden Street on Tuesday 25 April – he was one of several victims of a deranged British officer, Captain J. C. Bowen-Colthurst.

47 Éamonn Ceannt.

Lyons distinguished himself by the deadly accuracy of his fire, a certain enemy sniper who dominated one of our positions by his sharp shooting was soon silenced.[48]

Rifle and machine gun fire was continuous during the day only slackening towards nightfall when it became intermittent. The nights were sombre and awesome as we stood on guard we heard the noise of the improvised armoured cars as they raced around the side streets reconnoitring our position.[49] On Wednesday towards the middle of the week the firing increased in intensity, the crack of the artillery was heard above the rattle of machine gun fire and the loud bang of the Howth gun. The heavy guns of the British were in action, a red glare appeared in the sky, the General Post Office was on fire with incendiary shells. I could see the sky illuminated through the window whilst on night watch, the general attack was developing. What the result would be none then knew.

Watching the reflection of the burning city through that window, for by this time O'Connell Street was burning, listening to the constant booming of the Artillery, the smaller boom of the Howth gun, the sharp whisp-like report of the Winchester as snipers exchanged shots, I

48 According to Michael J. Molloy, who was on observation duty in Jacob's tower, 'The snipers claimed that the shining buckles of the British soldiers together with their bayonets showed them up very distinctly as targets' (BMH WS 716 p. 8).

49 Peadar Kearney wrote: 'They then tried improvised armoured cars … in which they would race up and down Aungier Street, firing volleys up Bishop Street; but as they had little time to steady their fire and the "rebel artillery" ('Howth' guns) were always ready for them, they got the worst of it and gave it up.' Quoted in de Burca, *The Soldier's Song*, p. 119.

discussed with Captain Dick McKee while on his inspection the probable outcome of events. Of one thing we were sure, the Home Rule Bill was dead, an end had been made of Parliamentary humbug on the question of Irish National self government. McKee who appeared more optimistic believed the Republic proclaimed on Monday would endure.[50] He was a fine specimen of a military officer, tall and dark-complexioned with a stern mien he impressed me as a man naturally adapted for military life. With his swinging parabellum automatic in his hand at New Street barricades, short crisp-toned orders, an alert look and well tailored uniform he inspired confidence as a leader. He struck me as a man not to be trifled with and of relentless, implacable purpose. Yet behind this exterior character was a frank and boyish disposition. A Lieutenant, he was promoted Captain in the Factory by McDonagh.

The night-watch in this corridor from the front gate to the Machine room was a lonely vigil before dawn. Gunfire had ceased for a while, with the exception of the interchange of a sniper, silence reigned. Watching the red glare in the sky, the burning city was to my rere, I surmised when the attack would be made on the spot where I was standing, as I glanced at the loaded Lee Enfield rifle that sharpened bayonet reminded me of frightfulness. I suppose many a soldier has ruminated on similar thoughts. Well, what the hell were we fighting for in any case? Can this damn thing

50 McKee went on to become commandant of the 2nd Battalion, but was later killed by the authorities in 1920.

called Freedom not be achieved in any other way? I was getting vexed. The red glow answered with a deeper hue. A burst of new gunfire announced the dawn, the attack had recommenced. It was now Thursday morning.

News was brought in that Captain Weafer had been killed defending Reis's building in O'Connell Street. Peadar Macken was shot fighting with De Valera at Bolands.[51] Many other casualties we heard of[,] the battle was increasing in intensity. Communications with the different commands was [sic] becoming more difficult. In this work of reconnoitring women were of invaluable service, they could pass where men were held up. The garrison was ever on the alert, we did not know the hour of attack or what would be done if the factory had to be evacuated. The Shelbourne Hotel we heard had been occupied by British troops and machine guns were spraying the College of Surgeons from the roof. We erected another barricade at a gateway leading to Bishop Street. In this operation I cut a finger and proceeded to the Red Cross first aid station in a square office in the middle of the ground floor. The station and hospital were under the supervision of Patrick Cahill, a chemist, assisted by Dick Davis.[52] Outside Pharmacies

---

51 Peadar Macken appears with de Brún in the photograph of the St Patrick's Day organisers in 1913 (see p. 22). Macken was accidentally killed by a fellow Volunteer at Boland's Mill on Thursday.

52 John MacDonagh recalled that when the rebels were lined up as prisoners in the square in Richmond Barracks, 'One man, Dick Davys [sic] who looked very important in his uniform, was asked by the famous detective, Johnny Barton … "Don't I know you?" "I know you," roared back the Volunteer, which answer got him put among the leaders and a long sentence as well' (BMH WS 532, p. 15). Although his witness

had provided through foragers surgical and chemical requisites to augment those found on the premises. After examination the tall and bearded Davis immediately took me in charge dressing the wound with almost professional skill. The Red Cross service here was ready for any emergency. Catholic clergymen came to hear confessions. I believe many of the men had the option of leaving and not a single man left.[53]

On Friday morning terrific fighting was taking place at Mount Street bridge[54] where enormous losses were inflicted on the enemy. De Valera was valiantly holding the British advance around Bolands Mill. Units of various sections in the factory were called out for a sortie.[55] We were paraded by Commandant McDonagh, who told every man to select a push bicycle from a heap of machines near by. I happened to select a first class one with a rifle holder and was pleased with my luck.

The Commandant then addressing us said – 'De Valera is very hard pressed at Westland Row Railway Station and Boland's Mill. I am sending out a party to make a diversion and reinforce him, doubtless you will meet with opposition. If you encounter the enemy and find your retreat cut off, take possession of the nearest houses, and

statement is signed MacDonagh and Mac is used throughout, the cover sheet uses Mc for both John and his brother Thomas.

53 Presumably de Brún is referring solely to those men who needed to attend the Red Cross station on the ground floor.

54 The Battle of Mount Street Bridge took place on Wednesday.

55 The sortie actually took place on Saturday – see *A Sortie from Jacob's*, p. 134.

make the most of it. We must draw the attack off Boland's Mill.' Young Lieutenant O'Riordan was placed in command of the party which numbered about twenty men. From this address we gathered our mission was a hazardous one. Some one suggested a cup of tea, it was preparing nearby, the Commandant acquiesced. He was a very approachable man in this respect. Indeed the spirit of officers and men was redolent of comradeship and cheeriness. Although the responsibilities of the situation were heavy on Commandant McDonagh no sign of this appeared in his demeanour.

We gathered our ammunition together, threw off all surplus stock and left by the Whitefriar Street exit. Since Monday it was the first time I was outside the building. It was the early morning and it was with a feeling of exhilaration I dropt the smell of the stuffy Factory. The weather was ideal. I thought of the proposed holiday that might never come off. On a morning like this any adventure could be attempted, perhaps that is why attacks start so fiercly [sic] at dawn. This feeling seemed to permeate the men. O'Rourke had two long feathers sticking out of his cap like an Indian Brave.[56] We chaffed him as we sped up Leeson Street. We passed a barricade at the Russell Hotel, Stephen's Green, without interference from the

---

56 The 1916 Roll of Honour lists two O'Rourkes (John and Michael) as well as an O'Rorke and two Ó Ruaircs. However, Volunteer Michael Joseph Lawless, who was in Jacob's, mentions a John O'Rourke of Seville Place, making him practically a neighbour of de Brún's. Given de Brún's apparent familiarity with the O'Rourke he mentions, it's likely that it was John O'Rourke.

Shelbourne Hotel and without mishap. We went through Pembroke Street, turned into Fitzwilliam Square and then into Fitzwilliam Street. At Baggot Street corner one of the brother Walshes (Jack) was put in charge of a Red Cross man as a precaution. We heard a section of the Red Cross were assisting the British. We cycled down Merrion Street when suddenly from the north end of Merrion Square we came under fire. Khaiki [*sic*] clad men from Mount Street ran to the roadway dropt on their knees and blazed away, others from round the corner of the Square fired through the railings. O'Riordan yelled 'take cover'. We jumped from our machines. There was little cover to take. I got possession of an electric tram standard in the middle of the road. Others got to railings and doorways, in fact there was precious little cover. The British troops I believe they were part of the raw recruits hurried from England to the attack on Mount Street. However, it was evident our objective, Westland Row Railway Station, would not be reached without being trapped and surrounded. O'Riordan gave an order to fall back. We remounted our machines, some covering the retirement until we were all in motion. An unconsciously humorous episode occurred here. O'Riordan, when we were taking cover, roared to one who took what he considered the best cover on the road, though paradoxically the most exposed, 'Ay so and so, get away from there, do you want to be shot?' One would imagine a manoeuvre rather than a battle was taking place.

We sped back, our short arms at the ready, this time through Fitzwilliam Street to Leeson Street Bridge via

Leeson Street to Stephen's Green past the Shelbourne hotel without a single shot, through the Russell Hotel barricade to the west side of the Green. As we rounded the corner towards York Street machine gun and rifles sounded with infernal din. We came under heavy fire from the top of Grafton Street. The Shelbourne and College of Surgeons came into direct action. Every post in the vicinity engaged. A breeze of bullets whizzed by us. I thought, and one thinks quickly in those situations, we would never turn York Street corner. Proud's lane is a near turn, I zig-zaged my bicycle to dodge snipers. Towards the lane some one comes up swiftly on my left, I swerve out to the middle of the road, deliberately slow I must widely turn into York Street and I do. Some one is hit. It's O'Grady. I think he came up on my left. We fall back as a rearguard while he is taken to the factory. When we reach there he is lying wounded in the groin and shin, poor fellow the pallor of death is in his face. The Red Cross are attending him. But for the covering fire of the College of Surgeons we would all be shot to pieces. Many of the Company went through Cuffe Street.

Commandants McDonagh and McBride eagerly question us on the sortie. McDonagh evidently satisfied exclaimed: 'Audacity's the thing!' Audacity's the thing!'[57]

---

57 French revolutionist Georges Danton, in a speech in 1792, said 'Il nous faut de l'audace, encore de l'audace, toujours de l'audace!' – We must dare, dare again, always dare! A variation is sometimes cited as a favourite quote of US Army General Patton: 'L'audace, l'audace, toujours l'audace' – 'Audacity, audacity, always audacity!'

By this time the Insurrection was well advanced. We hear that Eamon Ceannt was still stoutly defending his position in the South Dublin Union, Ned Daly causing havoc on the North side. The Imperial Hotel was being consumed by fire. Throughout the country the movement was spreading. The big guns could be heard from every direction. Most of our news arrived by courier. We were not aware of the growing superiority of the enemy. The remainder of the day passed on fatigue duty.

Saturday, St Patrick's Park was occupied by British troops. People had evacuated the houses in the neighbourhood. We expected attack any moment. The Adelaide Hospital was preparing for evacuation. The issue for the Garrison was rapidly approaching. Rumours came thick and fast. Communications were becoming more difficult to maintain. We chatted with people through the wired windows in Bishop Street. We were told Archbishop Walsh was trying to arrange a truce.[58] There was a cessation of gunfire, yet we stood to arms. The suspense was noticeable. We heard Commandant McDonagh had called to see Pearse and that the General Post Office was burnt out.[59] Carrying the wounded, this garrison was fighting its way to other positions.[60] If our position was shelled we would

58 Archbishop of Dublin William J. Walsh.
59 When Pearse's surrender order was delivered to MacDonagh, he refused to recognise it as binding, since it had been given while Pearse was a prisoner. He then went under a flag of truce to confer with Pearse in person.
60 When the GPO went on fire, the garrison evacuated to buildings on Moore Street.

likely have to fight our way to the Dublin Mountains and probably join up with contingents from Wicklow, Wexford, Carlow and other centres. Would our ammunition last out? I had over 60 rounds of rifle and a share of revolver stuff. These and other speculations ran through our minds. Only Headquarters Staff knew the actual situation as it stood then.

We were informed Commandant Pearse was in conference with General Maxwell and favoured surrender. The other Republican leaders were opposed, McDonagh particularly. Two Capuchin Clergymen were actively intervening, Fathers Albert and Augustine. Whilst the pourparlers were on we took advantage of the lull. By Sunday morning I had grown a stubble of beard I was anxious to remove.[61] I was rejoiced to find a comrade who possessed a new safety razor. He lent me the instrument, which I still possess as a souvenir. I removed the surplus hair and incidentally removed sections of my chin as well. It was the first and last time I used a safety razor. Commandant McDonagh had now returned and a conference was taking place of all the Senior Officers at staff headquarters on the ground floor. This lasted some time. After the conference all ranks got an order to parade at Headquarters. Two cowled clergymen were present, Fathers Albert and Augustine. Commandant McDonagh looked very serious as did most of the staff. Addressing

61 A rough growth of beard could have been a giveaway out on the street, so it's possible that de Brún was already considering his options when he decided to shave.

the Parade in a broken voice he told us 'that he had been in Communication with Commandant General Pearse and other General Officers. They had discussed the progress of the Republican forces during the week. They had come to the conclusion that a splendid assertion of Irish Independence had been gallantly made by the Army and its supporters, noble sacrifices had been made in the cause of Irish Freedom. Having regard to all the circumstances Commandant General Pearse was convinced that further sacrifice of life would be futile. With the welfare of the Irish people and the Army at heart he had decided to cease hostilities. He had agreed with the Commander of the British Forces, General Maxwell, to surrender on the guarantee that the men of the Irish Republican Army be treated as prisoners of war. Here McDonagh broke down and sobbed bitterly as did many of the officers and men. Some one asked what would happen the Commandant and other Leaders. McDonagh replied that for himself he did not know but he was assured the lives of the men would be safe. Father Augustine here intervened and said he was present at the conference with General Maxwell and was assured the Army would be treated as prisoners of war. There were loud cries of dissent amongst the men against surrender. Many were crying fiercely and shouting, 'Fight it out!' 'Fight it out!' 'We will fight it out!' Dick McKee was most vehemently opposed to surrender. Volunteer O'Malley[62] – a tailor by trade – loudly demanded to 'fight

---

62 The 1916 Roll of Honour lists a Christopher O'Malley in Jacob's.

it out', brandishing his shot gun. The Senior Officers, Commandants McBride and Hunter, were silent. They were resigned to the inevitability of surrender. Some one said the garrison was to march out carrying their arms and flags as prisoners of war. I was with Commandant Hunter after the parade broke up. He also wept bitterly with disappointment at the end of the struggle. Many of the men smashed their guns on the steel floors rather than surrender them to the British. Numbers of the men were given the option to escape from the building and availed of it.[63] The majority marched with their officers under arms to the internment camp to the Castle Yard and thence to the Richmond Barracks. The Factory was then taken over by a detachment of the Dublin Fusiliers and by a curious coincidence as one brother left the factory in the Republican ranks another marched into it in the uniform of the British Army. Looking back with some knowledge of the organisation of the different forces of the Dublin Brigade in the various areas of activities during Easter Week, it is evident that though all the other units of command were incessantly fighting, defending and consolidating their positions, though the General Post Office was the most important position and here the heaviest fighting occurred around O'Connell Street, Jacob's factory and its environs was the scene of military activities during the Week, the importance of which, I

63 Among those availing of the option, of course, was de Brún himself, but unfortunately he doesn't mention how the Rising ended for him – see *Escape from Jacob's*, p. 146.

believe, has not yet been realized in connection with the whole story of the Rising. The more one knows of the splendid organisation, of the complete state of defence, of the order and discipline that emerged after the first two days of occupation, of the many raids and sorties made from the Garrison, of the factory's adaptibility [sic] for supplying the needs of troops and the population on the south side of the city, with bread and flour should the emergency arise, and it did arise, the more one recognises the importance of Jacob's factory in the general plan of the Rising. The part played by Cumann na mBan in its defence and domestic organisation, of the Fianna Boy Scouts in its espionage system, when the whole story of the different parts of the factory is collected, it will prove that Commandants McDonagh, McBride and Hunter and their staffs achieved in a short space of time a state of efficiency under their commands and controlled activities which were and would have been of more vital importance had the Rising been prolonged and Dublin held for a longer time. As it was the garrison adequately served the needs of the Dublin Brigade as they arose during the eventful week in the area which it commanded and operated, to my mind and I write, not because I was of the garrison, but, rather because I know of the part played in its contribution to the History of Ireland at this momentous period. I desire to record my version of this epic week and to place the credit for its achievement as far as Jacob's factory is concerned to the memory of the brilliant and practical minds of the Commandants of the 2nd Battalion of the Dublin Brigade of the Irish Republican Army who directed this area of the Brigade's activities.

Signed: Seosamh de Brún
Date: 22nd October 1949

A Sortie from Jacob's

To the great frustration (but no doubt relief in some cases) of the men in the Jacob's garrison, their position saw very little military activity during the course of the rebellion. Some outlying posts were in action early in the week (mostly against irate local residents) before being withdrawn back to Jacob's, and some sniping was carried on from the high points of the building, while a number of Volunteers got to venture out on foraging trips in the vicinity. In the main though, the position was quiet – too quiet. One historian described Jacob's as a 'biscuit-filled mausoleum'.[1] We know too that the garrison had access to a designated rest area, with books and a piano, as well as a supply of clothes, boots and tobacco.

However, it's too simplistic to read these facts on paper and conclude that the rebels in Jacob's had an easy week – true, they weren't being shot at as much as other garrisons, but the reality, as we can see in de Brún's diary, was that the men had entered the factory prepared for a fight and thereafter experienced the stress and constant tension of awaiting an attack that never came. After one guard duty, de Brún writes: 'Suspense, tension. Darkness & silence save for the rattle of rifles & machine guns. Machine guns seem to be distinctive. Plug. Plug. Plug ... Guard ended, not

1 Charles Townshend – *Easter 1916, The Irish Rebellion*, London, Penguin Group, 2005.

fearsome but highly strung, can't sleep expecting attack, which does not come'. He may not have been in action, but given that he was writing 'on the spot', it's clear that Jacob's was not a place of relaxation.

One morning before the rebellion ended though, a small number of men got the opportunity to experience real danger, and for one of them it turned out to be the last experience he ever had. On that morning, a party of armed cyclists were assembled in Jacob's for a special task outside the factory. There have been references to this sortie in various books and magazines over the years, and it features in at least ten of the witness statements given years later.[2] But when it comes to hard facts, there's a wide variation among the accounts – what day the sortie took place, what its purpose was, how far it got, etc.

However, with de Brún's diary as a new primary source, we're able to clear up a lot of the discrepancies, and we can even name at least eight of the Volunteers who participated. When the men of the Jacob's garrison were giving their witness statements to the Bureau of Military History, at least three decades had passed, and so factual errors were almost to be expected. Yet within just two years of the

2   A tantalising reference to rebel cyclists is also contained in a diary kept by Lady Eileen Chance, who lived at 90 Merrion Square: 'Friday - [The maids] have returned safely. ... The poor girls walked to Ballsbridge for bread, and have been sitting up at the corner of Merrion Street all the morning ... While they were sitting there a batch of Sinn Féiners passed on bicycles, flitting back and forward silently like moths, and disappeared into Hume Street.' Quoted in O'Farrell, *1916. What The People Saw*, p. 153.

Rising, one printed history – the *Catholic Bulletin* – was mistakenly saying the sortie was on Thursday. The same day has been given in many histories since then, including *An tÓglách* in 1926, Desmond Ryan's *The Rising* in 1949, and the *Capuchin Annual* in 1966. Indeed, de Brún himself misremembered the day twice, giving it as Friday in both his 1937 and 1949 statements.

Nevertheless, it was early on Saturday morning,[3] 29 April, when fourteen men[4] assembled in Jacob's – some were selected and others volunteered.[5] Their mission was to cycle from the factory towards the Mount Street Bridge/ Boland's Mills area, and create a diversion to relieve pressure on Éamon de Valera's 3rd Battalion. It seems that word had gotten through from de Valera's command that his men were under pressure and expecting an attack. De Brún, whose description of the sortie in his statement is by far the longest and most detailed, quotes Commandant MacDonagh as saying: 'De Valera is very hard pressed at Westland Row Railway Station and Boland's Mill. I am

3 Some of the other participants also misremembered – Michael Walker initially said Wednesday. As a part explanation for these, and other discrepancies, it's interesting that Thomas Pugh wrote: 'The days were all mixed up because we had got very little sleep and we did not know one day from another' (BMH WS 397, p. 6).

4 Again, a variety of numbers were recalled by the participants and other garrison members – from as few as twelve to as many as twenty.

5 Among them were Seosamh De Brún (selected); Lt Dan O'Riordan; William James Stapleton (volunteered); John [?] O'Rourke; Michael Walker (selected); John Walker (selected); John O'Grady (who we know had his own bicycle, so was probably selected); and Jack Walshe (probably John Walsh, as listed in the Jacob's Roll of Honour; the Roll also lists a Patrick Walsh, who may have participated in the sortie).

sending out a party to make a diversion and reinforce him, doubtless you will meet with opposition. If you encounter the enemy and find your retreat cut off, take possession of the nearest houses, and make the most of it. We must draw the attack off Bolands Mill.' Although written decades later, this is remarkably reminiscent of what de Brún wrote in his diary on the same day as the sortie took place: 'selected to form "Diverting party". De Valera at Westland Row hard pressed.' And in his 1937 pension statement, under 'Particulars of any military operations', de Brún entered 'sortie to relieve and reinforce Commandant de Valera "hard pressed at Bolands Mill".' The last part is written in quotation marks, so it's clear that MacDonagh's words made a strong impact. The *Catholic Bulletin* in 1918 said that the purpose of the mission was to 'attack the piquets and drive them in on reaching Merrion Square, and, if successful, to connect with Boland's'.[6]

Command of the party was given to Lieutenant Daniel Reardon of 'C' Company.[7] Some of the rebels had brought their own bicycles to Jacob's, including Michael and John Walker, both of whom were champion cyclists and 1912 Olympians. For those without their own though, according to de Brún, 'Commandant McDonagh ... told every man to select a push bicycle from a heap of machines nearby. I

6 The *Catholic Bulletin*, September 1918.
7 Referred to in various accounts as Danny O'Riordan, Dan Riordan, or Dan Reardon. De Brún refers to him as 'young Lieutenant O'Riordan', while the Jacob's Roll of Honour lists him as Domhnall Ó Riordain. Nevertheless, in his own application for a military pension, the man refers to himself as Daniel Reardon, and gives his rank as Volunteer.

THE MILITARY SUNBEAM

An example of the type of military bicycle available in 1916. This Military Sunbeam cost £10 in 1915, but the rifle clips were extra!
Author's collection

happened to select a first class one with a rifle holder and was pleased with my luck.' Then, realising that they were about to set out on a dangerous mission, de Brún recalled that 'Some one suggested a cup of tea, it was preparing nearby, the Commandant acquiesced.'

The men then gathered up their ammunition, left behind whatever wasn't needed and set out. The weather was fine apparently and no doubt they were glad to be out of the mausoleum – de Brún wrote that 'with a feeling of exhilaration I dropt the smell of the stuffy Factory'. Again, the descriptions of the route vary, but it seems that, having left by Whitefriar Street, the column of cyclists crossed Aungier Street, and went up York Street to St Stephen's

Green. Turning right towards the Cuffe Street corner, then continuing along the south side of Stephen's Green, they went along Leeson Street and turned into Pembroke Street. They cycled down as far as Fitzwilliam Square, which they turned into, and then left down Fitzwilliam Street. Crossing Baggot Street, they continued along Fitzwilliam Street. Given how many British troops had poured into Dublin by the Saturday, and particularly given the casualties the troops had suffered at nearby Mount Street Bridge just three days earlier, it's remarkable that not only were the rebel cyclists able to leave Jacob's en masse and unseen, but that they managed to travel so far without being challenged.

Their luck ran out when they finally encountered some soldiers. De Brún remembered that 'suddenly from the north end of Merrion Square we came under fire. Khaiki [*sic*] clad men from Mount Street ran to the roadway dropt on their knees and blazed away, others from round the corner of the Square fired through the railings.' William Stapleton had a different memory: 'When we got as far as the corner of Merrion Square and Upper Mount St. we saw a British sentry at the corner of Lower Mount St. and we immediately opened fire ... Our fire was effectively returned by a strong fusilade of rifle fire from, I think, the building now forming Holles St. hospital.'[8] However, de Brún's diary states tersely: 'Soldiers at end of Sqr. Dismount opened fire'. His statement adds: 'O'Riordan yelled "take cover". We jumped from our machines. There

8   William James Stapleton, BMH WS 822, p. 7.

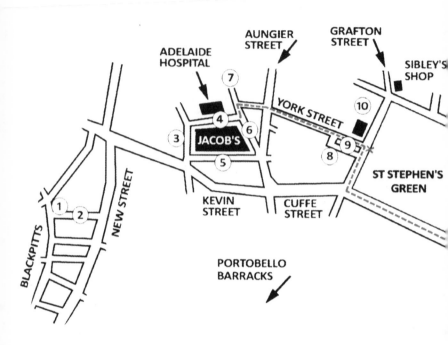

1. BARMACK'S

2. FUMBALLY'S LANE

3. BRIDE STREET

4. PETER STREET

5. BISHOP STREET

6. PETER ROW

7. WHITEFRIAR STREET

8. PROUD'S LANE

9. REBEL OUTPOST

10. COLLEGE OF SURGEONS

11. SHELBOURNE HOTEL

12. FITZWILLIAM SQUARE

13. FITZWILLIAM STREET

– – = Rebel cyclists' route

X = John O'Grady shot here

(GUIDE ONLY - MAP NOT TO SCALE)

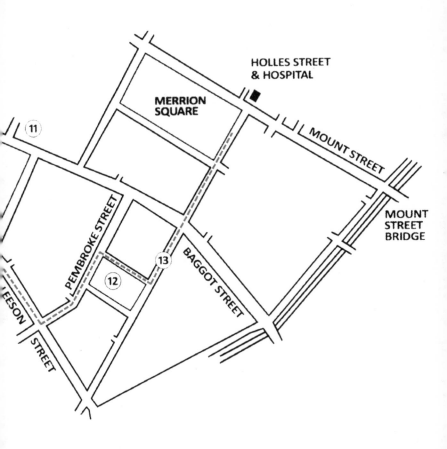

A map of the area of rebel activities in and around Jacob's factory in 1916. The dashed line indicates the route taken by de Brún and the other cyclists on their sortie from Jacob's early on Saturday morning, 29 April.

was little cover to take. I got possession of an electric tram standard in the middle of the road. Others got to railings and doorways, in fact there was precious little cover.'

The small party of rebels had done all they could – if reaching Boland's or Westland Row was their aim (as de Brún remembered), they had failed. But if creating a diversion and drawing the fire of the soldiers pressing on de Valera's positions was the aim, then they succeeded. An article by George A. Lyons (of the Boland's garrison) in *An tÓglách* in 1926 calculated that 'Consternation and dismay set in among the enemy. ... They redisposed themselves to face the changed situation and repel the new attackers. ... The diversion created by MacDonagh's men probably saved our situation ... '[9]

It was now time to leave – 'O'Riordan gave an order to fall back. We remounted our machines, some covering the retirement until we were all in motion,' recalled de Brún. Returning by essentially the same route, the cyclists got back as far as the Cuffe Street corner of Stephen's Green, when friendly shouts warned them that British troops were at the top of Grafton Street. Some of the party went up Cuffe Street, but others continued along the Green. To get to the turn into York Street though, the cyclists had to cycle directly towards Grafton Street for about 120 metres, and they instantly came under heavy fire – 'machine gun and rifles sounded with infernal din,' recalled de Brún. Seán Murphy, although not one of the cyclists, wrote later

9   *An tÓglách*, Vol. IV, No. 14, 17 April 1926, p. 3.

*The west side of St Stephen's Green, looking from the Cuffe Street/
Harcourt Street corner towards Grafton Street. The prominent building
with columns on the left is the College of Surgeons, with the entrance to
York Street just in front. It was here (approximately where the closest
cyclist in the photograph is) that Volunteer John O'Grady was fatally
wounded, probably by British soldiers located on the top of Sibley's shop
at the top of Grafton Street, which is directly along the tracks from the
position this image was captured.*

*This is one of a series of photographs taken in 1952 by an Army Air
Corps photographer, now in the Bureau of Military History's collection.
Each photograph has an annotation on the back written by Frank
Robbins, who served in the St Stephen's Green area with the Irish
Citizen Army. On this picture he wrote: 'The houses this side of the
College of Surgeons were occupied by Lieut. Robert de Coeur's section.
One of the men in his section was Liam O'Briain, now a professor in
Galway University.'*

Photograph reproduced courtesy of the Military Archives

that he thought the shots were coming from Sibley's shop at the top of Grafton Street.[10]

Some rifle fire from a friendly outpost started, which helped to cover the cyclists as they tried to reach York Street. This covering fire had been arranged beforehand, when, at the start of the sortie, Reardon had paused at a rebel outpost beside the College of Surgeons. The post (between York Street and Proud's Lane) was occupied by, among others, Liam Ó Briain, who remembered: 'He told us that he and his party were going to cycle round by Merrion Square "looking for fight" and would be returning via Stephen's Green South and York Street to their base in Jacob's factory ... He wanted us to open fire as soon as we saw them returning to "cover their retreat". ... I said "we will do that" and off they cycled bravely with their rifles strapped to their machines ... So we waited more than half an hour ... Suddenly shooting started quite near us, from our men, so we all opened fire all along our position ... The cycling party were just turning the corner into York Street and safety when the machine gun sputtered.'[11]

A Volunteer coming up on de Brún's left was hit. Calling to his officer, John O'Grady said: 'Dan, I fear they have got me.'[12] Reardon ordered some cyclists to support O'Grady on either side, and de Brún and others acted as a rearguard while he was taken back to Jacob's.

10 Sean Murphy, BMH WS 175, p. 8.
11 *The Capuchin Annual*, 1966, p. 232.
12 *Catholic Bulletin*, September 1918, quoted in Bateson, Ray, *They Died by Pearse's Side*, p. 152.

John MacDonagh, brother of Commandant Thomas MacDonagh, remembered: 'I had taken the names of the column before they went out, and was checking them on their return. I remember the anxiety of the wounded Volunteer to get his name and address in the list. His name was O'Grady. Tom sent across the street to the Adelaide Hospital for a doctor. The Volunteers were told that no doctor would come but any casualty sent over would be looked after. Tom sent them back to bring a doctor over by force. One did come, in a very bad temper, and announced that there was little hope for O'Grady. He assured us that he would get every attention in the hospital, so poor O'Grady was brought across and died almost immediately.'[13]

William Stapleton remembered that 'When we brought the wounded McGrath into the building there was considerable distress evident among the small party of girls from Cumann na mBan who were in charge of cooking and attached to the First Aid Station.'[14]

De Brún recalled: 'When we reach there [Jacob's] he is lying wounded in the groin and shin, poor fellow the pallor of death is in his face.' Joseph Furlong wrote that O'Grady 'was killed with a bullet in the stomach. It looked as if it was an explosive bullet as his stomach was practically ripped out.'[15]

---

13 BMH WS 532, pp. 11–12. Again, the accounts differ – one says O'Grady died six hours later, another that it was the next day.
14 BMH WS 822, p. 8. Stapleton has gotten O'Grady's name wrong. In fact, none of the accounts were able to supply O'Grady's first name – not even MacDonagh, who remembered how anxious O'Grady was to have his name and address recorded.
15 BMH WS 335, p. 7.

The Sinn Fein Rebellion Handbook includes the following information supplied by the Adelaide Hospital: 'During the rebellion there were admitted to the Adelaide Hospital the following: — Dead, soldiers, 4; civilian, 1; wounded, soldiers and civilians, 70, who received treatment and of whom four died of their wounds.' O'Grady would have been one of the four referred to.

According to the *Catholic Bulletin*, September 1916, 'John James O'Grady, twenty-seven years of age, was an ex-pupil of the Christian Brothers, Francis Street, Dublin, and for eleven years a member of the Third Order of Saint Francis, Merchant's Quay. He was married but eight months before the Rising, and though only four months a member of the Irish Volunteers he enjoyed the confidence and the friendship of his comrades to a remarkable degree.[16] On April 29th he was mortally wounded in the neighbourhood of Jacob's Factory – being represented as the only casualty in that area – and he was attended at his death by F. Metcalfe.'

Volunteer O'Grady had a brother Charles who was also fighting in the Rising, with the Roe's Distillery Garrison. In a statement he gave to the Bureau of Military History in 1949, Charles J. O'Grady recalled his journey home on Sunday morning: 'I went on down towards my home and turned into Nicholas Place, and the first person I met was a D.M.P. man's daughter. She stared at me and came over

16 A report from the Office of Director of Intelligence in 1924 stated that O'Grady joined the Volunteers in 1913, and subsequently 'took an active part during the gun-running at Howth'.

and said "Thank God you are alive. I am sorry about your brother". This was the first I heard of my brother's death. He was a volunteer of A/Coy. Battn. III. – John O'Grady – and had been killed on Saturday morning at the corner of York St. He was one of a party of cyclists from Jacob's garrison ... This party was commanded by Dan Reardon, C/Coy. 2nd Bn. My brother died in the Adelaide Hospital and is buried in James's Churchyard, James St.'[17]

Author Ray Bateson concludes O'Grady's story: 'According to a member of the [O'Grady] family, he was buried in St James's Churchyard because the British were paying particular attention to funerals and his brother [Charles] was on the run.'

In 1923 Josephine O'Grady wrote to the Ministry of Defence in application for a pension 'as the widow of the late John J. O'Grady who died on the 29th April 1916 at the Adelaide Hospital from bullet wounds received on that date while serving with the National Forces in Jacobs factory'. The date of their marriage was given as 30 August 1915. The Army Pensions Board approved the application, and because O'Grady was killed during the Rising, his pensionable rank was established as 'Officer'. (In February 1932 Josephine was remarried, to a man called John Caffrey.)

17 BMH WS 282, p. 7.

ESCAPE FROM JACOB'S

As we've seen in both his diary and later witness statement, Seosamh de Brún was silent on the subject of how the Rising ended for him. However, we do know that his name doesn't appear on the published prisoner lists, and he doesn't seem to have been arrested or even questioned in relation to his participation in the rebellion.

So it's easy to deduce that at some point on Sunday, the day the Jacob's garrison surrendered, de Brún left the body of men preparing to surrender and slipped away – within weeks he was back at his contracting work, operating from his base in No. 9 Lower Exchange Street and possibly even repairing some rebellion-damaged buildings.

But how unusual was it for a rebel from Jacob's to successfully avoid capture? In fact quite a number of the garrison's 200 or so did slip away undetected, and at least five witness statements held by the Bureau of Military History are by Volunteers who describe their escape, and who occasionally name other escapees. Another Volunteer who got away was Peadar Kearney (author of the lyrics for the Irish national anthem), who didn't leave a witness statement, but did, however, leave a detailed account of his experiences (published posthumously).

When news of the decision to surrender was relayed by Commandant MacDonagh to the rank and file of Jacob's on Sunday, two things happened in quick succession. The men of the garrison were, in general, bitterly disappointed, and reacted in different ways. Eamon Price recalled 'a scene of incredible pandemonium and confusion. Men, old in the movement, seeing their dearest hopes dashed to the ground became hysterical weeping openly, breaking their rifles against the walls.' Seamus Pounch remembered ruefully, 'I dumped my gun with the rest and it was the saddest parting I can remember.'[1]

Peadar Kearney was even more descriptive: 'When on Sunday Tom Hunter came down from Headquarters and drawing his sword he smashed the blade in two and announced with broken voice and tears in his eyes that surrender had been decided on, the scene that followed was beyond word painting. Fierce anger predominated, while the best of men collapsed and became temporary imbeciles. ... A man with a Belfast accent forced a rifle on me. I took it, not knowing his purpose. In a moment the poor fellow had his tunic unbuttoned and his shirt torn open. "Here," he cried, "shoot me! I'm not going to surrender".'[2]

Nevertheless, the men's disappointment and rage couldn't change the facts – the garrison was surrendering, like it or not. The next consideration for each man then, was whether he should surrender with the garrison, or try to get away and take his chances in the streets. It's important to remember that there was a real fear among the rebels that they would all be executed for their part in the Rising. Many of them turned to their leaders for advice.

1   Eamon Price, BMH WS 995, p. 2; Seamus Pounch, BMH WS 267, p. 13.
2   Quoted in de Burca, *The Soldier's Song*, p. 127.

From MacDonagh, two different answers are recorded – the majority saying that he advised escape. Thomas Slater and Michael Hayes (among others) recalled that MacDonagh 'told every man that could to get away as there was no use of lives being lost';[3] and that he also said 'that those who had no uniforms had permission to get away if they could'.[4]

On the other hand, Thomas Pugh's memory of Mac-Donagh's advice was exactly the opposite: 'As MacDonagh made the point that it would be a kind of desertion of the leaders not to surrender in force, I said that as I came out under orders I would do whatever I was ordered to do.'[5] He remained with the garrison.

However, other leaders and advisers also counselled escape. Michael Walker recalled that 'Another clergyman entered the premises through a window and urged all who could to escape from the building.' Walker then wrote: 'My brother John and myself approached Capt. McKee and I told him I believed we could make our escape. He shook hands with me and said "More luck, Mick, if you succeed let my mother know I am safe". I promised to do so.'[6]

Again, Kearney's recollection is more picturesque: 'I decided that I had no intention of marching to Bride Street to give myself up ... But while determined to make a bid for the open, I did not care to do so without inducing

3 Thomas Slater, BMH WS 263, p. 22.
4 Michael Hayes, BMH WS 215, p. 5.
5 BMH WS 397, p. 7.
6 BMH WS 139, p. 7.

some of my close comrades to do likewise. One man said he would not desert his leaders, another that it wasn't worth while, and another that the idea was hopeless. [One good friend of Kearney's was Thomas Pugh, who decided to surrender.] Precious time was being lost in arguing when Major MacBride came along ... I called him; he immediately came over and the problem was explained to him ... "Liberty is a precious thing," he said, "and any one of you that sees a chance, take it. I'd do so myself, but my liberty days are over." ... That settled it and half-a-dozen of us faced the streets of a hostile and fear-stricken city.'[7]

Even decades later though, there seem to have been some mixed feelings over the decision of some to escape. Éamon Price wrote: 'I advised the very young lads and the older married men with dependent children who were not in uniform to try to get away. I must say that not all took that course but stuck manfully to their officers.'[8]

Despite the advice to the contrary though, the majority of the garrison remained in the factory and surrendered together – but what of those who decided to chance an escape? A number of them were in Volunteer uniform, which posed an obvious 'visual' problem, but it's difficult to know how many of the garrison turned out in uniform that day. On the way to Jacob's, William James Stapleton noted that 'Quite a number of the men were in Volunteer

7 Quoted in de Burca, *The Soldier's Song*, p. 128.
8 BMH WS 995, 'The Surrender of Jacob's Garrison', p. 2.

uniforms.' But Joseph Furlong remembered differently, saying: 'Very few of our men were in uniform.'[9]

In the event, some men were able to discard their uniforms and don civilian clothes while still in the factory[10] – in de Brún's diary, he mentions that there were 'Plenty of new clothes, boots' available.[11] Others, however, braved the 100 or so metres to a nearby priory. Michael Walker recalled that 'Many who [escaped] were supplied with clothes which had been left by people at the Whitefriars St Priory.' Brothers Mick and Thomas Slater also shed their uniforms in the priory. Other rebels risked going even further while still in uniform – Seamus Pounch 'got as far as Camden St. where I was met by a young Fianna member ... who invited me to his home, as troops were at Harcourt

9   William James Stapleton, BMH WS 822, p. 4; Joseph Furlong, BMH WS 335, p. 8.
10 The National Museum holds a Volunteer tunic found in Jacob's and donated to the museum in 1917.
11 The supply of clothes to the garrison had a poignant echo in the 1940s. Two sisters, Mary and Anne Reynolds, who found themselves falling on hard times, were in correspondence with the Taoiseach's office seeking an extension in the employment of Anne, who was due to be let go from her job in the Department of Social Welfare. The women's brother, George Reynolds, had died while commanding the rebels at the battle of Mount Street Bridge, and Taoiseach Éamon de Valera approved a payment of £100. But when that was running out, the sisters wrote again, this time including the detail that in 1916: 'We ourselves had a clothing establishment in Redmond's Hill and supplied many of the men in Jacob's Factory during Easter Week with clothes for which we never received a penny.' *Thom's Directory* of 1917 records '1-3 Redmond's Hill: Reynolds, M. & A., clothing boots and shoes, furniture and miscellaneous property dealers.' The value put upon the goods they supplied was £100, and Anne's employment was subsequently extended to December 1947. It's unknown what their subsequent fate was.

Road and I could not possibly reach Charlemont St. in uniform and I was wearing puttees.'[12]

The escapees' experiences (and methods) varied greatly – young Vincent Byrne recalled that 'James Carbury and myself were brought along ... to a low window in Bishop Street and just dropped out into the street and told to go home.' Also going via a window was Michael Walker and his brother John, who 'left the building through a window and ... eventually succeeded in reaching home ... after a nightmare journey through the military lines.'[13]

Meanwhile, Thomas Slater wrote simply that 'a good lot of us cleared out and got away. ... I managed to get home and was never arrested,' while Michael Hayes left 'with Edward Byrne and Michael Cavanagh ... walked up Bride Street, Heytesbury Street to Lower Clanbrassil Street, where I lived. I was not interrogated or arrested subsequently.'[14]

According to Padraig Ó Ceallaigh, some rebels only seem to have made the decision to escape while they were actually marching towards surrender: 'We walked about half a mile before we met the British troops to whom we surrendered ... Before we reached the British, some of the boys just walked out into the crowd which almost lined the way to the point of surrender, and escaped. The leaders

12 Michael Walker, BMH WS 139, p. 7; Seamus Pounch, BMH WS 267, p. 13.
13 Vincent Byrne, BMH WS 423, p. 4; Michael Walker, BMH WS 139, p. 7.
14 Thomas Slater, BMH WS 263, p. 22; Michael Hayes, BMH WS 215, p. 5.

who included Thomas MacDonagh, Major MacBride and Michael O'Hanrahan could as easily have escaped.'[15]

Meanwhile, when Peter Cushen, a Jacob's employee, heard that the rebels had surrendered, he went to the factory, where he saw about ninety rebels emerging from the factory windows and 'the rabble' getting up the rope that was hanging from the office window and tumbling out sacks of flour. In the bakehouse, he saw about 100 of the rebels standing and sitting about. Rifles were lying on the floor, and picking one up he tried to halt the looters, but more got in through other windows. Later, he recalled that 'one of the officers of the rebels came into the office ... He said there was a lot of bombs stored away that would blow up the whole place, and as they had done no damage, they did not want the blame to be left on them if any careless person handled them. He brought me round and pointed them out to me, and we came back again and he showed me where there were some hand grenades stored in the little ovens ...'[16] Soon after, along with some other employees, Cushen neutralised eighteen hand-made bombs by placing them in a water tank. By 6 May, less than a week later, the managing director of Jacob's was able to report that production in the factory had already resumed.

Based on this account then, we can estimate that of the 200 or so members of the garrison, about half escaped. And although we can count de Brún among them, we'll probably

---

15 Padraig Ó Ceallaigh, BMH WS 376, p. 4.
16 As quoted in *W&R Jacob – Celebrating 150 Years of Irish Biscuit Making.*

never know exactly how he got away. Nevertheless, some detail is available – in a summary of evidence given in 1937 in support of his application for a military service pension, de Brún was asked, and answered, the following questions:

Q: What happened at the surrender – were you able to get away?

A: I was told to get away.

Q Who told you?

A: Comerford.

Q: Did you get away?

A: Yes; it was an indirect get-away.

Q: How did you manage it?

A: I just kept on walking.

Samuel Henry Lomas –
an autographed photograph, with a postcard back, undated.
Author's collection

'ABSOLUTELY FULL OF SINN FEINNERS'

An introduction to
Company Sergeant Major S. H. Lomas

Samuel Henry Lomas was born in November 1879 in the village of Tideswell, in Derbyshire, England, into the family of a coal agent and his wife and three daughters.[1]

Tideswell is a village within the UK's Peak District National Park, with a fairly constant population of about 2,000. In the UK's 1891 census, the eleven-year-old Lomas was living with his family on Church Street, and by the 1911 census, the now thirty-one-year-old was a quarry foreman living in nearby Bakewell, with his wife of six years, Sarah Ann, and two-year-old son William. In May 1913 Lomas was listed in *The London Gazette*,[2] having been appointed a Sub-Inspector of Quarries,[3] and a year later, he was listed again, now appointed an Inspector of Factories and Workshops.[4] However, this wasn't to be Samuel's last mention in the *Gazette*.

---

1 Information courtesy of http://places.wishful-thinking.org.uk/DBY/ Tideswell/DBY9125-2.html, accessed August 2013.
2 An official newspaper of record for the UK, in publication since 1665.
3 *The London Gazette*, 6 May 1913. S. H. Lomas is also included in the H.M. Mines Inspectorate list for 1913 as 'Sub-Inspector of Quarries, York & North Midland Division' (http://www.dmm.org.uk/hmim/ index_l.htm).
4 *The London Gazette*, 5 May 1914.

On 31 October 1914 Lomas enlisted in the Territorial Force, although he was no stranger to a uniform, having previously served nine years with the 2nd Volunteer Brigade Sherwood Foresters. And for his service in the Boer War (1899–1902), Lomas was awarded the South Africa medal.

In his new uniform, he was part of the recently raised 2/6th Battalion, The Sherwood Foresters, and his previous military experience was possibly responsible for his early rank of Company Sergeant Major (CSM). Thanks to a battalion history, we know that a Divisional Gymkhana and Sports Day was held in Luton on 16 June 1915, which saw the 2/6th Battalion tug-of-war team winning first prize – the eight team members' weights are given, and CSM Lomas was 14 stone, 11 lb. The history continues: 'Several members alas were killed on active service later.'[5]

Lomas was thirty-six years old when he set sail from the port of Liverpool, aboard the Royal Mail steamer *Ulster*, on the evening of Tuesday 25 April 1916. Less than twenty-four hours earlier, the Sherwood Foresters had been ordered to prepare for a sudden move from their location in Watford, Hertfordshire, about seventeen miles from London. The Foresters were part of the 59th Division; considered a 'flying division' and carefully situated near two main railway lines, with trains kept

---

5   Edmunds, G. J., *2/6th The Sherwood Foresters 1914-1918, Its Part in the Defeat of the Irish Rebellion 1916*. Edmunds was the officer commanding, 'A' Company, 2/6th Battalion, The Sherwood Foresters, and served with the regiment throughout the rebellion.

A photograph of the RMS Ulster, *taken in September 1920.*
Author's collection

ready at the stations and soldiers constantly practising rapid entraining.

The men had been granted Easter leave, but when orders came through for a move before dawn the next morning, 'all ranks were recalled from the cinemas and other places of amusement and in the middle of all the bustle and packing a Zeppelin raid warning was issued'.[6] Nevertheless, despite the short notice and the Zeppelin threat, the battalion's trains moved off on time, headed to Liverpool. Two transport ships were waiting, but room on board was limited, with the RMS *Ulster* having to take both the 2/5th and 2/6th Battalions – resulting, we're told, in the officers leaving behind their general kit and their saddle horses. More importantly, as

6   Edmunds, G. J., *2/6th The Sherwood Foresters 1914–1918.*

far as the coming week was concerned, the battalion's Lewis machine-gun units were also left behind.

The ship's destination was Kingstown (Dun Laoghaire) in Ireland, and for the next fourteen days CSM Lomas kept a diary of his time in Ireland. A typed transcript of this diary is now held by the UK's National Army Museum, but little is known about its background and unfortunately the whereabouts of the original (if it even still exists) are also unknown. As with all eyewitness accounts, particularly those written during periods of high stress and physical danger, it's not uncommon to find errors or flaws in the notes the writer has made (misnamed streets, for example). However, a diary containing daily entries written under battle conditions is rare enough – and one written while a rebellion was taking place is as rare again. This makes the contents of such a diary historically valuable enough that it is worth reading (and reproducing) in full, flaws and all.

The most obvious flaw in CSM Lomas' account is the inclusion of two full entries for Thursday 27 April. Both days are fully annotated, with specific times given for various duties. However, while this is curious, it is not difficult to find a possible explanation. Because we have no reason to doubt the authenticity of the typewritten diary, which was donated to the National Army Museum over twenty years ago, the error most likely occurred when the manuscript was being transcribed. Handwriting can sometimes be impossible to decipher, and we can presume at least that, given the circumstances, Lomas' notes were probably very difficult to make out. A note at the end of the typescript says

'Typed N.R.P.' , and just before that, it says: 'In copying the diary into type, times 'am' and 'pm' are in places confused.' Unfortunately, nothing is yet known about N.R.P., but errors or no errors, we can be extremely grateful to him or her for helping to preserve CSM Lomas' words.

Lomas was involved in some of the most intense fighting of Easter Week – he supervised the building of barricades across several important streets, including Parnell Street, he led storming parties to break into buildings around Moore Street, discovered the body of The O'Rahilly, and participated as senior NCO in the rebellion's first executions in Kilmainham Jail – those of Pearse, MacDonagh and Clarke. And although these are well-known events, as with all diaries, it's the first-hand accounts, and the discovery of new pieces of information, that makes them fascinating.

From Lomas' diary, we hear that although for Pearse and MacDonagh death was instantaneous, Clarke 'was not quite so fortunate, requiring a bullet from the officer to complete the ghastly business'. Intriguingly, we also hear that Pearse 'whistled as he came out of the cell'.

It was Lomas' service in Dublin which gained him his final mention in *The London Gazette* – he was listed for having been awarded the Distinguished Conduct Medal 'For conspicuous gallantry and devotion to duty. He erected barricades under very heavy fire and set a splendid example throughout.'[7]

7 *The London Gazette*, 23 January 1917.

Unfortunately by the time Lomas' diary ends, we know he had less than a year to live. He was one of the battalion's tug-of-war team who 'alas were killed on active service'. His Military History Sheet lists his service in France as beginning on 26 February 1917 and ending on 27 April 1917.[8] The Battalion War Diary for that day reads: '1am Battalion marched to Hargicourt Road to deploy prior to an attack on Quarries and Colagne Farm. The attack was launched at 3.55am and the Quarries were successfully captured and a line consolidated east of the Quarries. Seven prisoners and 1 machine gun were captured.' It seems that at some point during this action, CSM Lomas was killed, but his body was never recovered. With no known grave, he is commemorated on the Thiepval Memorial to the Missing of the Somme. Attached to his Military History Sheet is a receipt for the post-war medals that Lomas was entitled to – the British War Medal and the Victory Medal. It's signed by his widow, Sarah Ann.

Samuel Henry Lomas' name is also engraved on the war memorial in his home town, Tideswell: 'In ever loving memory of the men of this town who gave their lives for their country's sake in the Great War.' The memorial stands at one end of Church Street, where the eleven-year-

---

8   'On February 25th, 1917, the Division moved to France. The Brigade crossed from Folkestone to Boulogne and from the quays, the men in full marching order and kit had a gruelling march of two and a half miles uphill to the standing camp at the top. Here conditions were very poor …' Edmunds, G. J., *2/6th The Sherwood Foresters 1914–1918*.

old Lomas was recorded in the UK's 1891 census, in the town where he spent most of his life.

The war memorial in Tideswell, Derbyshire. Samuel Henry Lomas'
name is engraved on the memorial, which stands at one end of Church
Street, within sight of the house where he lived as a child.
Photograph courtesy of BazzaDaRambler

Transcript of the Personal Diary of 3415 Coy. Sgt. Major S. H. Lomas[1] 'D' Coy. 2/6 Battn Sherwood Foresters, 178 Infantry Brigade

Awaiting orders to prepare and embark for IRELAND in the troubles of 1916, at the half way stage of the First World War[2]

WATFORD

April 24th 1916 8.30pm Received orders to prepare for a sudden move.[3]

12 midnight. All packed and ready to move. Orders given that battalion would entrain at 5.30am.

April 25th. 1.30am Notified of a 'Hostile Air Raid'[4]

Piquet[5] paraded at 1.40 and stood to while required.

---

1 Transcript of the diary kept by Sgt Maj. S. H. Lomas, 24 April to 8 May 1916. National Army Museum Accession Number 1990-12-107. All original punctuation and spelling has been retained.

2 Although we don't know when the transcription was made, the use of the phrase 'First World War' by the typist shows that it was after 1918. We can't, however, assume it was made after the Second World War, since the two terms are recorded as having been used as early as 1939.

3 The Sherwood Foresters were considered a mobile battalion. 'The Easter holiday was a favourable opportunity for getting married … One of the grooms at Brigade Headquarters was married on the Monday night at Watford, and his honeymoon was rudely interrupted at midnight' – *59th Division 1915–1918.*

4 This is the Zeppelin raid mentioned in Edmunds' *2/6th The Sherwood Foresters 1914–1918* – see p. 157.

5 Picquet or picket: a soldier or small group of soldiers maintaining a watch.

5am Battalion paraded and marched to the Watford Junct. Station.

7.30am All troops and transport loaded.

7.50am Train moved out. Destination Liverpool.

2.10pm Arrived at Liverpool Dockside Station.

3.20pm Boarded the Royal Mail steamer ULSTER for Kingstown.[6]

3.50pm Moved off from the dock and after an uneventful journey sighted the harbour.

9.30pm All troops on board consisting of the 5th and 6th Btns Sherwood Foresters disembarked and were marched to the Town Hall Square, Kingstown.

10.30pm Two days rations were issued to the men and a market porters handcart commandeered to carry 4000 rounds of ammunition and surplus rations.

April 26th 1916 1am Battalion moved off in the direction of Dublin.

2am Arrived at an industrial school for boys 1½ miles from Kingstown.[7] The whole of the Battn were allowed to use the dining room and school room to sleep.

5.30am Reveille. Men very tired but quite cheerful.

6 It's well documented that when some soldiers arrived in Dun Laoghaire, they assumed they'd landed in France, even trying some French phrases on the locals. However, the officers and NCOs weren't as uninformed. 'Later that morning when the morning papers could be procured, we learnt that Casement had been arrested in Ireland. We then knew our destination.' Edmunds, G. J., *2/6th The Sherwood Foresters 1914–1918*.

7 This was most likely Carriglea Park, an industrial school on Kill Avenue, Dún Laoghaire, operated by the Christian Brothers between 1894 and 1954.

8am. The whole place cleaned up, all the Battn paraded in company's in the playground ready to move off. An additional 20 rounds of ammunition per man issued, making 140 rounds per man.

9am. Moved out through Kill en route for Dublin. 'D' Coy on the right flank. The country was difficult to make much headway, owing to the many houses requiring searching.[8] Owing to dykes and high walls we got out of touch with Battn.

3pm On arrival at Black Rocks, we found our Battn had gone on.[9]

3.30pm After a short halt we proceeded towards Donnybrook.[10]

5pm We left Donnybrook and kept on the outskirts of Dublin. Marched towards Wellington Barracks.[11] The people who we passed along the street were exceptionally kind, giving tea, water, food, cigarettes at scores of places.

6pm. Owing to the majority of the men being so tired, the Captain decided to go into the Barracks for a short halt. The soldiers stationed there were the Royal Irish Rifles, and provided us with tea. We were able to eat our bully and biscuits with comfort and safety.

8   G. J. Edmunds in his book *2/6th The Sherwood Foresters 1914–1918*, said of this: 'The men found it very exhausting work to examine houses and grounds but stuck to their tasks splendidly.'
9   Blackrock, about 5km (3 miles).
10 A distance of about 3km (2 miles). Marching from Dun Laoghaire to Donnybrook via Kill Avenue and Blackrock is not the most direct route.
11 Now called Griffith Barracks, on the South Circular Road. It closed as a barracks in 1991.

6.30pm We resumed our march towards the Royal Hospital.[12] We could hear the firing in the distance but we were not troubled.

7.50pm We arrived at the Royal Hospital.[13] After unloading our rifles we were allowed to take up our quarters for the night in the corridors, thoroughly tired out.[14]

27th April 1916. 5.30am. Reveille. Cleaned up the rooms, had breakfast and paraded in the quadrangle at 10am – full fighting strength – After standing by for two hours we received instructions to move.

12 oclock noon. Marched out from the Royal Hospital en route for Dublin Castle.[15] All along the road, constant sniping was going on but the Royal Irish, by keeping up a constant fire in the direction of the snipers, prevented them from

12 The Royal Hospital Kilmainham housed the British military head-quarters in Ireland and was home to the army's commander-in-chief, Ireland.

13 'Sniping was going on continuously from the South Union Workhouse held in force by the rebels and from which their flag flew. This place was about 600 yards from the Hospital. Posts here returned the fire of the rebels and several bodies under the walls spoke to the accuracy of the shooting.' Edmunds, G. J., *2/6th The Sherwood Foresters 1914–1918*.

14 Edmunds writes that the officers slept in the church, adding: 'The Church of the Royal Military Hospital is a beautiful building, with many fine paintings and much Gibbons carving, but as a night resort it proved distinctly chilly.' Nevertheless, it was probably more comfortable than the corridors.

15 Dublin Castle was the seat of British government in Ireland: 'up in the Keep a strong body of troops was keeping sustained fire on the Four Courts and snipers on the roof tops. One good shot was credited with having accounted for 72 snipers but was himself killed on the last day. All the time the ping of bullets on the walls of the Castle continued. The enemy was certainly not short of ammunition.' Edmunds, G. J., *2/6th The Sherwood Foresters 1914–1918*.

concentrating their fire on the column. We arrived at Dublin Castle without any casualties.

2pm Had dinner and a short rest.

3pm Four parties of 20 men each and an officer were selected from 'B' Coy, and four from 'D' Coy. The eight parties were allotted to me.

5pm This was cancelled for 'D' Coy. 'B' Coy having moved out in an armoured car, and taken up positions in houses at the corners of streets, breaking in the doors when necessary to take up the positions.[16]

6pm. 'D' Coy were ordered to proceed along Cappel Street,[17] Parnell Street to consolidate the position held by the Royal Irish. We moved out and on crossing the bridge over the

16 This entry records one of the earliest ever uses of armoured personnel carriers. Five improvised armoured cars were designed and constructed in haste just the day before, in response to the situation in Dublin. The raw materials consisted of Daimler lorries borrowed from Guinness's brewery, as well as a number of locomotive boilers and a quantity of steel plate. Two different designs were built – one was made from four boilers placed together to form a single curved enclosed space, and the other was a more straightforward arrangement of flat steel plates, forming a box-like structure. Slits were made in the armour surrounding the cab for drivers to peer through, while loopholes were cut into the sides, both for air to come in and for soldiers to fire out of. Dummy holes were also painted alongside, to confuse the enemy. Accommodating as many as twenty-two troops, according to one account, the interior of both designs must have been extremely uncomfortable: 'The noise of the rifles in such a confined space was stupendous' (Gibbon, Monk, *Inglorious Soldier*, p. 64). Typically, the contraption was backed up to a target building, with a machine gun laying down suppressing fire if necessary. A party of troops carrying crowbars and axes would then jump out and secure the building. Edmunds wrote that when buildings were secured, 'the task of picking off snipers who hitherto had had it all their own way was carried out with gusto.'

17 Capel Street.

*One of the hastily constructed armoured cars put together in response
to the rebellion and made from locomotive boilers and steel plates,
with loopholes cut into the sides for soldiers to fire out of. Although poor
quality, this is a rare photograph, clearly showing both the real rifle slits
and the false ones painted on to confuse the enemy.*
Photograph reproduced courtesy of the Military Archives

river from Parliament Street,[18] we came under heavy fire from the Sein Feinners [sic].[19] We proceeded up Cappel Street and on entering Parnell Street, at every cross street we were subjected to rifle fire from the enemy.

On arrival at Moore Street, I was instructed to make a barricade right across the street.[20]

18 The bridge is Capel Street Bridge, also called Grattan Bridge.
19 'As we emerged from the Castle and crossed Grattan Bridge the bullets whizzed round, a heavy fire coming from the Four Courts. Bullets struck the parapet and the tram lines and ricochetted, throwing sparks in all directions. But the troops were very cool and unafraid.' Edmunds, G. J., *2/6th The Sherwood Foresters 1914–1918.*
20 Edmunds writes that when the armoured car had secured all the corner buildings, 'the companies marched out into the streets and were given instructions to barricade all side streets, and entries on either side of Capel Street up to the junction with Sackville Street.'

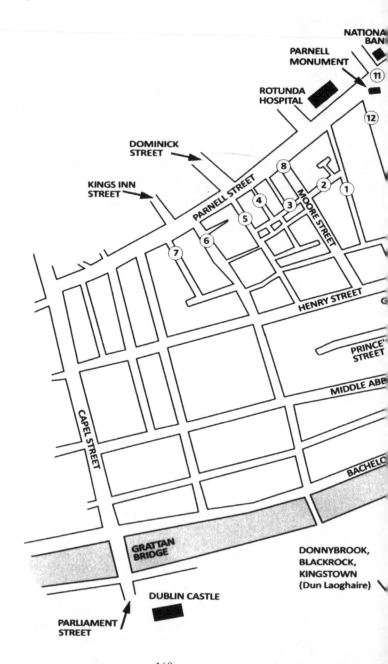

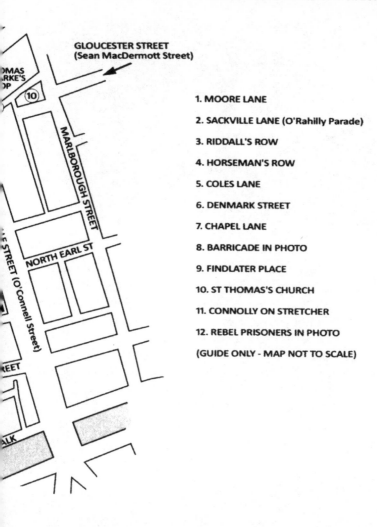

1. MOORE LANE

2. SACKVILLE LANE (O'Rahilly Parade)

3. RIDDALL'S ROW

4. HORSEMAN'S ROW

5. COLES LANE

6. DENMARK STREET

7. CHAPEL LANE

8. BARRICADE IN PHOTO

9. FINDLATER PLACE

10. ST THOMAS'S CHURCH

11. CONNOLLY ON STRETCHER

12. REBEL PRISONERS IN PHOTO

(GUIDE ONLY - MAP NOT TO SCALE)

A map of the area in central Dublin where CSM Lomas was in action in 1916, including where most of his diary entries were written.

In his diary, Lomas wrote: 'On arrival at Moore Street, I was instructed to make a barricade ... proceeded to make the barricade assisted by 12 men. To find material for this, the furniture of a butcher's shop was used consisting of blocks, bedding, stands, wardrobes, spring mattresses etc.' Many of these items are clearly visible in this photograph of the barricade outside Simpson & Wallace, Victuallers & Contractors, located at 57 Great Britain Street, particularly the butcher's block on which one soldier is lying, while resting his rifle on a metal bedstead. It was this barricade for which Lomas was awarded his Distinguished Conduct Medal: 'For conspicuous gallantry and devotion to duty. He erected barricades under very heavy fire and set a splendid example throughout.' And it was this barricade that The O'Rahilly and his men were charging when they met a hail of bullets. Author's collection

7.30pm Proceeded to make the barricade assisted by 12 men. To find material for this, the furniture of a butcher's shop[21] was used consisting of blocks, bedding, stands, wardrobes, spring

21 Simpson & Wallace, Victuallers & Contractors, located at 57 Great Britain Street (now Parnell Street) (www.lennonwylie.co.uk/1913 PhoneList13.htm – accessed September 2013).

mattresses etc.[22] This barricade was completed by 11pm and three sentries were posted. We were then instructed to make safe all the barricades of 'D' Coy consisting of seven at the various streets, viz:– Coles Lane, Denmark Street, Kings Inn Lane, Chapel Lane and two streets the names of which I did not take.[23] When this was completed we got over the barricades and fixed three lots of trip wires, to hold up the enemy in case of a rush. During the whole of the time incessant firing was being carried on by both sides.[24] Whilst the barricade at the end of Moore Street was being erected, a picked squad of Royal Irish held positions on house roofs and in top storey windows, effectually preventing an attack.

27th April 1916. 2 am. The work being made as safe as possible, I found an armchair used for the barricading, and so slept peacefully until 5.30am.

5.30am Relief guards sent on duty, barricades further strengthened, additional men allocated and breakfast given out.

22 'Much ingenuity was displayed in closing streets with any material that could be procured.' His own 'A' company procured a number of sacks from a nearby soap factory off Parnell Street in order to make 'sand bags' – 'The poorest houses in the streets had nothing on the ground floors but 'mother earth', so the men were set to with their entrenching tools to hack up the soil and fill the sacks.' Edmunds, G. J., *2/6th The Sherwood Foresters 1914–1918.*

23 Many of these streets and lanes no longer exist, having disappeared in 1981 with the opening of the Ilac shopping centre. Coles Lane and Denmark Street ran between Henry Street and Parnell Street. Kings Inn Lane is misnamed and should be King's Inn Street. The two unnamed streets could be Lower Dominick Street and Granby Row.

24 It seems likely that it was this action for which Lomas was awarded the Distinguished Conduct Medal: 'For conspicuous gallantry and devotion to duty. He erected barricades under very heavy fire and set a splendid example throughout.'

9.30am An 18-pounder was brought up. A fatigue party was then taken to remove the setts to provide a place for the shovel of the gun.[25] This was at the corner of Coles Lane. Four shells were fired down the street into a large shop at the bottom in Henry Street,[26] in which Sein Feinners were making explosives. Messrs Curtiss & Sons, Brass Foundry and Munitions Factory.[27] This must have upset their calculations somewhat, as the firing from that direction almost ceased. The plate glass windows in the locality were shattered by the explosion of the charge, and the shell cut through the factory like a knife.

12 noon. Nothing further of interest to note, with the exception of one man getting wounded in the arm, whilst engaged in trying to snipe a sniper.

6pm Sniping became more incessant until dark. All extra men were mounted and posted. Inspected by the O'C Coy.[28]

10pm The men rolled up in their blankets (those standing by) and tried to get a little sleep but without much success, as

25 Setts are the rectangular stones used for paving roads – often mislabelled as cobblestones.
26 This shop was most likely Arnotts store, which in 1916 lay directly opposite Coles Lane. Edmunds quotes a Sergeant Andrews: 'the corner house on Parnell Street, which I occupied, was facing Arnots [*sic*] Building in Henry Street. ... On the Friday, about noon, an 18 pounder gun fixed up against my barricade and fired a number of shells into Arnots building.' Edmunds, G. J., *2/6th The Sherwood Foresters 1914–1918*.
27 Lomas seems to have been given incorrect information as to the shop's name. W. Curtis & Sons, Manufacturers of Brass and Copper Work, had premises nearby on 98 & 99 Middle Abbey Street, but not on Henry Street.
28 Captain W. E. V. Tompkins was Officer Commanding (OC) 'D' Company.

everything was so cold, and one blanket not sufficient to keep you warm.

28th April 1916. 3am. Daybreak. Men procured buckets from the houses, washed & shaved and got breakfast. Yard brooms were borrowed and the whole street cleaned up.

10am The men were allowed to rest in the sun when not on duty, taking care to have cover from the snipers in the locality.

12 noon One 18-pounder arrived and laid facing down Moore Street in the direction of the G.P.O. Four shells were fired which caused the rebels to quake, as for some considerable time, the rifle fire was silent, with the exception of a few snipers.

Note. The artillery proved most useful, & were in my opinion mainly the cause of the surrender of the rebels.

The machine guns, Lewis type, also did excellent work, and any hope the rebels had of making a rush was quelled before it was hardly thought of.

6pm Sentries and piquets posted and checked, additional guards provided.

7pm Trouble by a man several times coming to the barricades, he being full of beer.[29]

29th April 1916 Saturday 12.30am Made a visit to all posts and found the men alert and attending to their duties.

1am Turned into my blanket until 5.45am.

---

29 A medical orderly described 'a Dressing Station in Parnell Street at a public house. Their first case was a civilian, who though challenged several times by a sentry would not stop and was shot in the thigh. He died later.' Edmunds, G. J., *2/6th The Sherwood Foresters 1914–1918*.

These images are part of a collection of photographs taken during the Rising by Second Lieutenant Milligan of the Royal Irish Rifles. Each is printed on a postcard backing, on which Milligan helpfully wrote a descriptive note. On the top photograph is written: 'Officers of 5th Rifles in Findlater Place', while on the one below it says: '5th Royal Irish Rifles in Findlater Place taken on Friday 28th April 1916'. On 28 April the rebellion was nearing its end, but the fighting in the Sackville Street area was at its most intense. The rebels had evacuated the GPO and fought their way to buildings on Moore Street. Lomas wasn't far away from these soldiers when he wrote: 'The men were allowed to rest in the sun when not on duty, taking care to have cover from the snipers in the locality.' Milligan thought to record the moment, turning his camera left to photograph the officers on one side of Findlater Place and right to take the soldiers on the other.

Photographs reproduced courtesy of Karl Vines

6am morning ablutions. Same street, same place, very cold, rather frosty.

6.30am Breakfast (ham and eggs, bread and a lovely cup of tea, dont know where they came from – for information see batman. I know he and his pal were in the confined area by dawn[)].[30]

9am Received instructions to prepare for storming parties of 20 men and an officer, and to provide ourselves with tools of any description to break down the doors etc. To search the houses through to Henry Street and to make a breach when necessary in the walls.

12.30pm All ready and the assault commenced. My party were allotted to an alley with houses either side. My weapon was a bar 5'6" long 1½" strength with a lever end – a beautiful tool for the purpose. I struck at one door such a smack and knocked the door complete for some 5 yards into the house, breaking hinges and lock at the same time. Sweating like the devil! (Rather with fear, excitement or work) It is surprising how the lust to destroy comes over you.[31]

---

30 'The Foresters' skill in making the best of any situation was shown here by Lieut. Maine's batman ('B' Company), Private Charnley. He found a little shop in a basement. The occupants made them welcome to all they had in the way of food (for which they were handsomely recompensed) and we managed to get hot tea and a good breakfast for our men in place of the despised bully-beef and biscuits.' Edmunds, G. J., *2/6th The Sherwood Foresters 1914–1918*. Perhaps not the same man, but the Commonwealth War Graves Commission lists a Private F. Charnley of the 1/5 Battalion, Sherwood Foresters, as a fatality in France on 29 March 1918.

31 'A' Company was ordered to clear Denmark Street – 'Carefully searching all the houses as we pushed on, we found a rabbit warren of alleys on the east side. The women were incoherent with fear and what with hysterical

2pm Orders are passed for us to stand by as a white flag was approaching the end of Moore Street. This was found to be from Sean O'Connelly asking for terms of surrender.[32] Instructions were sent back up the street for O'Connelly to come down and interview the General in command of our troops. This was done, O'Connelly being carried down on a stretcher, as he was wounded in the leg. Whilst standing by, we came across the dead body of O'Reilly, the acting adjutant.[33] This man was shot on the Wednesday evening previously by one of our sentries (FT) and had managed to crawl into Moore Lane and die.[34] There were two more Sein Feinners near to, but we were unable to identify by any papers they

women, screeching children and the unpleasant task of searching the filthiest houses one had ever seen, the task was anything but pleasant.' Edmunds, G. J., *2/6th The Sherwood Foresters 1914–1918*.

32 Lomas is referring here to James Connolly, commandant general in charge of Dublin operations, who was wounded badly in the ankle and did indeed require a stretcher.

33 Lomas' information isn't entirely accurate: the body he's referring to seems to have been that of M. J. O'Rahilly – The O'Rahilly – who led a charge out of the GPO towards Moore Street on Friday 28 April. He was killed by machine-gun fire from the barricade at the top of Moore Street whose construction Lomas had supervised. Edmunds writes: 'Lieut. Brace with 80 men manned the barricade opposite the Post Office and had a reserve party well protected from sniping. This platoon broke up a strong enemy attack from the Post Office …' Edmunds, G. J., *2/6th The Sherwood Foresters 1914–1918*. If this refers to O'Rahilly's party, then their small number was many times outnumbered and clearly never stood a chance of success. Aodogán O'Rahilly, in his biography of his father, *Winding the Clock*, writes (p. 222): 'The British officer in charge of the barricade was a Captain G. J. Edmunds' (presumably Brace's superior officer) who said that he had "sent a sergeant to search O'Rahilly's body" and "we found some interesting papers on him". Among the papers was a farewell note to his wife, which included the line "I got more than one bullet I think".'

34 O'Rahilly actually died in Sackville Lane, which joined Moore Street and Moore Lane – it has since been renamed O'Rahilly Parade.

*On the back of this Milligan photograph is written '489 prisoners taken
in G.P.O. & surrounding buildings on Saturday evening 29th April
1916 about 6 p.m. Prisoners drawn up & being searched in Sackville
St.' The soldiers are wearing full backpacks, and there are so many of
them, it's hard to make out any individual rebels. The photograph was
taken at the north end of Sackville Street. The building on the right,
just to the left of the tree, is the Rotunda Hospital. The buildings visible
on Sackville Street are No. 40, Crane and Sons Ltd, pianoforte and
organ merchants; No. 39, Kelly, Brothers & Co., Wine Merchants (and
upstairs, the United Irish League); No. 38, J. Purcell, cigarette factory;
No. 37, Dawson & Co., booksellers, stationers and importers of fancy
goods. The rebels were later marched to the Rotunda Gardens, where they
remained overnight.*

Photograph reproduced courtesy of Karl Vines

possessed.[35] About 7am[36] the whole lot of the rebels decided
to surrender[37] and to see them troop out of the house in

35 One of these was Volunteer Paddy Shortis, a twenty-three-year-
old native of Ballybunion, County Kerry. The other could have been
Volunteer Patrick O'Connor from Rathmore, County Kerry.
36 This must be 7 p.m.
37 Edmunds writes that 'a little fair-haired Irish nurse came in to the

*The map opposite was included as part of the transcribed diary, and takes
up a full page. The correct names have been added here in grey. We can
assume that it was most likely hand drawn by Lomas in his diary and
copied by N.R.P. Unsurprisingly it's not an accurate map of the area,
and some notations don't seem to make sense when compared to a formal
map. For instance, Denmark Street was in fact parallel to Moore Street.
However, if we consider that Lomas probably meant Dominick Street,
and we bear in mind that when he wrote about O'Rahilly's body being
found on Moore Lane, he was actually referring to Sackville Lane, then
the map starts to make sense. Across Moore Street from where Sackville
Lane ends there was another small street called Riddall's Row, before it
met Cole's Lane, and this was intersected by an even smaller lane called
Horseman's Row, which joined it to Parnell Street. This is probably the
'Alley' referred to in Lomas's drawing, which means 'our position' was
a spot opposite Horseman's Row. Riddall's Row and Horseman's Row
disappeared under the Ilac Centre development in 1981.*

Moore Street between three and four hundred of them. The
several storming parties were ordered to stand by just in time,
as the next house we were about to enter from the back, 36
Sein Feinners came out of the front.[38] Part of these men were
marched up to the Rotunda and there searched, and part we
searched.[39] 100 men of one Battn were told off as escort. The

Colonel's headquarters, with a flag of truce (with a large red cross on it),
and asked for terms for the Sinn Féiners. She was most pleasant to talk
to … but told us little …' This was Elizabeth O'Farrell.

38 This entry seems to place Lomas and his storming party in Moore Lane,
which ran behind the houses in Moore Street.

39 'The 2/6th Battalion played an important part in disarming the hundreds
of men packed in the small space of the Post Office that was not on fire.
All kinds of weapons were taken from the men and piled high in the
streets.' Edmunds, G. J., *2/6th The Sherwood Foresters 1914–1918.*

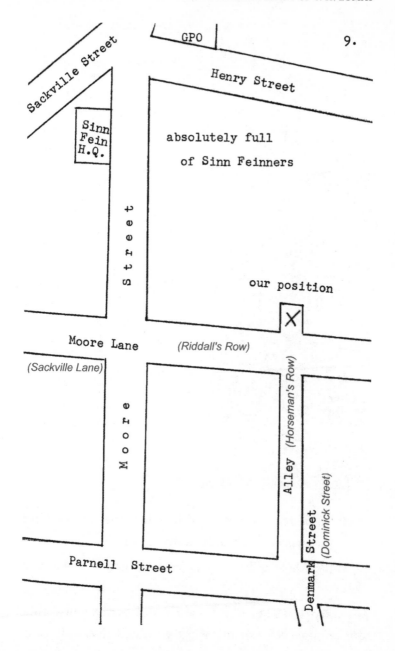

On the back of this Milligan photo is written 'Sinn Fein Rebel captured in Gloucester St. Wednesday 26th April 1916' (now Seán McDermott Street). This rebel is heavily armed, but we do not know whether he was captured with all of his weapons, or whether he was re-armed for the sake of the camera. He is holding the Howth Mauser with fixed bayonet – most likely one of the German Mauser Model 1871/84 single shot 11mm rifles landed in Howth and Kilcoole in 1914. Although large, heavy and cumbersome, the Howth Mauser could be a very efficient weapon in the right hands. He is also wearing an ammunition bandolier and has a small pistol tucked into what looks like a string belt. The other item on his belt looks too small to be a scabbard for the bayonet, and may be another bladed weapon. Photograph reproduced courtesy of Karl Vines

whole of the rebels were corraled on the green for the night at the Rotunda Hospital under a strong guard.

10pm the whole of the barricades were again manned until morning.

30th April 1916. 6am Breakfast was served and then a tour of inspection was made in the vacated area, and it was noted what a lot of looting had been done either by the rebels or by the people in the slum area adjoining.

Sackville Street appeared to be a mass of ruins, and dead men were being gathered in from all directions. The whole of the day was spent on this class of work, all the houses being searched for dead and arms.

8pm The same vigilance was again used as on the previous night, all the barricades being manned.

1st May 1916. 6am Breakfast

9am Battn paraded and marched via Sackville St to Dublin Castle. All available troops being massed on the Green, General Sir John Maxwell inspected and addressed the troops.[40] Thanking them for services rendered etc.

1.30pm Marched off to the Royal Hospital via Phoenix Park. No duties were found and the men were allowed to get a rest for the night.

2nd May 1916. Reveille at 6am. The whole of the morning was devoted to a general straightening up. 'B' Coy were sent to Richmond Barracks.[41] 'A' Coy to Haydon Bridge Barracks.[42] Our Coy were detailed for duty consisting of 90 men and NCO's.

9pm I was warned to provide a party of 48 men and 4 sergeants for a special duty parade at 3am the following morning.

---

40 This was College Green, opposite the main entrance to Trinity College Dublin.

41 'B' Company were sent there 'to take charge of the prisoners and their effects'. Edmunds, G. J., *2/6th The Sherwood Foresters 1914–1918*.

42 This seems to be a misnamed reference to Islandbridge Barracks, renamed Clancy Barracks after independence.

I was told as a special favour I had been allowed to go as one of the party as senior NCO.[43]

43 From the notes following, it seems conclusive that Lomas was senior NCO at the execution of the first three rebel leaders on 3 May 1916. The identities of the men who carried out the executions of the fifteen rebels in 1916 were never officially recorded, but some information has become known since then. One officer who commanded a firing squad on 8 May left a memoir – Captain Arthur Annan Dickson of the 2/7 Battalion, The Sherwood Foresters. His recollections were written in the early 1920s, not long after the events in Dublin in 1916: 'I was to march my firing-squad of a Sergeant and 12 men to a space cut off from the execution-point by a projecting wall; halt them to ground arms there; march them forward 12 paces to halt with their backs to their rifles, each of which I was then to load and replace on the ground. Thus no man knew whether his rifle had been loaded with blank or with ball; each was therefore left not knowing whether he personally had shot the man or not. The men were then [to be] marched back to pick up their rifles and hold them, at attention under my eye, until word came that the prisoner was to be led out; they must then be marched round and halted facing the execution wall. We marched our squads to [Kilmainham Jail] long before dawn in a dismal drizzle ... We had to wait while it grew faintly light and I took the chance to instruct the squad exactly what orders they would get; I didn't want any muddle ... After "Ready!" I told them, "on the word 'Present,' you bring your rifles smartly up to the standing-aim position, aiming at a piece of white paper pinned on his chest and on the word 'Fire' – steady pressure on the trigger, just like on the range. Then, at once, I shall give you 'Slope arms' – 'About turn'; then as we clear this wall – 'Right incline' – 'Halt' – 'Ground arms'." Thanks to that preparation, it was carried out smoothly. The 13 rifles went off in a single volley. The rebel dropped to the ground like an empty sack ... I can't say I felt much else except that it was just another job that had to be done ... I was glad there was no doubt the rifles had done their work and there was no need for me to do what [an] old Major had told me, about the officer going back and finishing the job off with his revolver' (quoted in O'Farrell, *50 Things You Didn't Know About 1916*, pp. 124–6). It's interesting to note that Lomas was asked to provide forty-eight men and four sergeants – enough for four firing squads, although only three executions were carried out that morning. Perhaps there were originally four executions scheduled and the orders were changed, or perhaps one squad was kept in reserve for unforeseen circumstances.

The officer being Lieut Rogers of 'C' Coy.[44] 'C' Coy were ordered to provide 12 men and a sergeant with shovels for a fatigue parade at the same time and proceed to the Detention Barracks.[45]

May 3rd 1916. We paraded at the time appointed, marched to Kilmainham Jail.

At 3.45 the first rebel MacDonoghue was marched in blindfolded, and the firing party placed 10 paces distant. Death was instantaneous.[46] The second, P.H. Pierce[47] whistled as he came out of the cell (after taking a sad farewell of his wife).[48] The same applied to him. The third J.H. Clarke, an old man, was not quite so fortunate, requiring a bullet from the officer to complete the ghastly business (it was sad to think that these three brave men who met their death so bravely should be fighting for a cause which proved so useless and had been the means of so much bloodshed).[49]

5am – This business being over, I was able to return to bed for two hours and excused duty until noon.

---

44 The Commonwealth War Graves Commission lists a Lieutenant Stanley Arthur Rogers, 2/6 Battalion Sherwood Foresters, as having died in France on 21 March 1918.

45 It's possible that these men were detailed to dig the mass grave in which the executed rebels were buried.

46 Thomas MacDonagh, Proclamation signatory and commandant 2nd Battalion Dublin Brigade, based in Jacob's factory. MacDonagh was Volunteer Seosamh de Brún's commanding officer.

47 Patrick H. Pearse, Proclamation signatory, commander-in-chief of the rebel forces and president of the Provisional Government.

48 In fact, Pearse wasn't married, and was only visited by a Capuchin priest, Fr Aloysius, who heard his last confession. It's intriguing, however, to read a report that he whistled as he left his cell.

49 Thomas J. Clarke, Proclamation signatory.

*On the back of this Milligan photograph is written 'Sinn Fein Officers
taken prisoners Saturday 29/4/16'. Although Milligan didn't name
him, we can be confident that this is the only known, and previously
unpublished, photograph of James Connolly taken during the Rising.
Connolly lies wounded on the stretcher, flanked by six of his own men,
and surrounded by at least fifteen British soldiers, with more just out
of frame. The photograph was taken at the very north end of O'Connell
Street, probably in front of the Parnell monument. All the men are facing
into Parnell Street, and on their left is Cavendish Row. On the large
building, we can just make out 'National Bank Ltd', which was No. 165
Parnell Street (still largely intact today). The shop with the sign that
says 'Hair' is No. 163, a hairdressers under the name of J. G. Ridgeway,
and the premises just in front, No. 164, was run by M. Graham, sub-*

*postmaster, stationer and bookseller. Directly opposite the National Bank
on Parnell Street was a premises Connolly would have known well – the
tobacconist shop run by Tom Clarke. CSM Lomas, in his diary entry for
the afternoon of Saturday 29 April, mentions Connolly 'being carried
down on a stretcher'. The incident involved a party of rebel Volunteers
and officers carrying Connolly from Moore Street under a flag of truce to
a temporary British HQ in the National Bank, where the stretcher was
laid down by the Parnell monument. Shortly after, the order was given
to carry Connolly to Dublin Castle. Several witness statements given to
the Bureau of Military History describe the event in detail, including
those of Diarmuid Lynch (BMH WS 4), Liam Tannam (BMH WS
242) and Michael Staines (BMH WS 284).*

Photograph reproduced courtesy of Karl Vines

2pm We again found all duties and were again posted.

8pm The whole of our Coy. were withdrawn and instructions given that 'C' & 'D' Coys., were to proceed to Longford the following morning, and from there to be sent to the west of Ireland as No.1 Flying Column.[50]

May 4th 1916. Reveille 3am

Parade 5am

Arrived at Broadstones (?) Station 6am.[51]

Entrained for Longford at 8am. Arrived Longford 12.30pm[52] Proceeded to the Barracks which we found occupied by about 200 King Edward's Horse, 'D' Coy was allotted the Riding School. Squadron Sgt. Major Poston kindly offered to share his bunk and the whole of the sergeants were cordially welcomed. The whole of the staff were exceedingly kind to us, making our stay with them very enjoyable. In particular I may mention S.S. Major G. Poston late 16th Lancers, Saddling Sgt Fleshman, a saddler from near London and Acting Quartermaster Sgt Bennett who belonged to the C.I.V. in the Boer War.[53] We spent a pleasant evening with them.

50 Edmunds writes: 'Generally speaking the column was well received by the people and no resistance of any kind was met. A certain amount of arms and ammunition was captured and a few Sinn Féin prisoners were arrested and sent to Richmond Barracks.'

51 Lomas was almost correct – Broadstone railway station, on Constitution Hill on Dublin's northside, was the former Dublin terminus of the Midland Great Western Railway.

52 A postcard sent from Longford in May 1916 by a soldier in the 2/6 Foresters noted: 'We have had an awful time of it, but thank goodness it is all over now.'

53 C.I.V. = City Imperial Volunteers, a unit that fought in the Boer War (1899–1902). Lomas was also a veteran of that war.

May 5th 1916. The whole of the day was spent in inspections, issue of ammunition etc and again had an enjoyable time in the mess and finished up at 2.30am at peace with the world.

May 6th 1916. The day broke with rain in torrents, which continued the whole of the day. Our orders were to stand by ready to move if the rain stopped. We passed most of our time in the mess, with the exception of a walk out with several of the sergeants into the village of Longford to see some of their friends. Got to bed about 12 midnight.

Sunday May 7th 1916. Reveille 5.30am Still raining. Had breakfast and paraded at 7.30am. Marched off 8am for Roscommon 22½ miles away. We had rain all the way and very cold, and after an uneventful journey arrived at Roscommon 5.30pm. Very tired and stiff. Billets were allotted and we secured any [sic] empty house using the breakfast room for Jim and I with our batman. After visiting the picquets and seeing that they had received their food, I returned to our billet at 9pm, ready for bed.

8th May 1916. Monday. All equipment was dried and the day up to noon spent with inspections of feet, rifles and any boots requiring repairs were attended to. In the evening I went to look at the Roman Catholic Church (Roscommon), built of black stone, and found some fine carving, both in wood and stone, making it a beautiful place altogether.

———————

[The following was entered by the person who transcribed Lomas' diary.]

The diary ends here and is followed by sketchy memoranda on various matters.

(In copying the diary into type, times 'am' and 'pm' are in places confused)

Typed

N.R.P.

REFERENCES

Bureau of Military History Witness Statements (BMH WS)

Peadar Bracken, BMH WS 12 and BMH WS 361

Fergus (Frank) Burke, BMH WS 694

Vincent Byrne, BMH WS 423

Sean Cody, BMH WS 1035

Seosamh de Brún, BMH WS 312

Joseph Furlong, BMH WS 335

Seamus Grace, BMH WS 310

Michael Hayes, BMH WS 215

John J. Keegan, BMH WS 217

Margaret Kennedy, BMH WS 185

Diarmuid Lynch, BMH WS 4

John M[a]cDonagh, BMH WS 532

Henry McNally, BMH WS 49

Michael J. Molloy BMH WS 716

John J. (Sean) Murphy, BMH WS 204

Liam O'Briain, BMH WS 565

Padraig O'Kelly [Ó Ceallaigh], BMH WS 376

Charles J. O'Grady, BMH WS 282

Seamus Pounch, BMH WS 267

Eamon Price, BMH WS 995

Thomas Pugh, BMH WS 397

Frank Robbins, BMH WS 585

Thomas Slater, BMH WS 263

Michael Staines, BMH WS 284

William James Stapleton, BMH WS 822

John J. Styles, BMH WS 175

Liam Tannam, BMH WS 242

Michael Walker, BMH WS 139

Charles Wyse-Power, BMH WS 420

Military Service Pensions Collection

Seosamh de Brún: File reference MSP34REF846 (Joseph Brown)

Select Bibliography

An tÓglách: The Army Journal, Vol. IV, 1926

Bateson, Ray, *They Died by Pearse's Side*, Irish Graves Publications, Dublin, 2010

de Burca, Seamus, *The Soldier's Song: the story of Peadar Kearney*, P.J. Bourke, Dublin, 1957

Capuchin Annual, The, Dublin, 1966

Catholic Bulletin and Book Review, The, M.H. Gill, Dublin, 1916–1917

Edmunds, G. J., *2/6th The Sherwood Foresters 1914–1918, Its Part in the Defeat of the Irish Rebellion 1916*, Wilfred Edmunds Limited, Chesterfield, ND [1960]

59th Division 1915–1918, Wilfred Edmunds Limited, Chesterfield, 1928

Gibbon, Monk, *Inglorious Soldier*, Hutchinson & Co. Ltd, London, 1968

Hopkinson, Michael (ed.), *Frank Henderson's Easter Rising*, Cork University Press, Cork, 1998

London Gazette, The, The Stationery Office Limited, London, 1913, 1914, 1917

Morrissey, Thomas, 'Saving the Language: "The Impatient Revolutionary"', in *Studies: An Irish Quarterly Review*, Vol. 77, No. 307 (Autumn, 1988), pp. 352–7

Nic Shiubhlaigh, Máire, *The Splendid Years*, James Duffy & Co. Ltd., Dublin, 1955

O'Farrell, Mick, *A Walk Through Rebel Dublin 1916*, Mercier Press, Cork, 1999

O'Farrell, Mick, *50 Things You Didn't Know About 1916*, Mercier Press, Cork, 2009

O'Farrell, Mick, *1916 – What The People Saw*, Mercier Press, Cork, 2013

Ó Maitiú, Séamus, *W&R Jacob: Celebrating 150 Years of Irish Biscuit Making*, The Woodfield Press, Dublin, 2001

O'Rahilly, Aodogán, *Winding the Clock: O'Rahilly and the 1916 Rising*, Lilliput Press, Dublin, 1991

Reilly, Tom, *Joe Stanley: Printer to the Rising*, Brandon, Dingle, 2005

Royal Commission on the Rebellion in Ireland, *Report of the Commission*, 1916

Ryan, Desmond, *The Rising*, Golden Eagle Books, Dublin, 1949

Sinn Féin Rebellion Handbook, Easter 1916, compiled by the *Weekly Irish Times*, Dublin, 1916

Thom's Official Directory, Alex. Thom & Co. Limited, Dublin, 1916, 1917

MERCIER PRESS

IRISH PUBLISHER - IRISH STORY

We hope you enjoyed this book.

Since 1944, Mercier Press has published books that have been critically important to Irish life and culture.

Our website is the best place to find out more information about Mercier, our books, authors, news and the best deals on a wide variety of books. Mercier tracks the best prices for our books online and we seek to offer the best value to our customers, offering free delivery within Ireland.

A large selection of Mercier's new releases and backlist are also available as ebooks. We have an ebook for everyone, with titles available for the Amazon Kindle, Sony Reader, Kobo Reader, Apple products and many more. Visit our website to find and buy our ebooks.

Sign up on our website or complete and return the form below to receive updates and special offers.

www.mercierpress.ie
www.facebook.com/mercier.press
www.twitter.com/irishpublisher

Name:

Email:

Address:

Mobile No.:

Mercier Press, Unit 3b, Oak House, Bessboro Rd, Blackrock, Cork, Ireland